Christopher Miele

Hoxton

*Architecture and history
over five centuries*

A HACKNEY SOCIETY PUBLICATION

Published by The Hackney Society
115 Eleanor Road, London E8 1DN

Copyright © The Hackney Society 1993

Designed and printed by Expression Printers Ltd
London N5 1JT

Cover *Pitfield Street Library, 1896. Designed by Henry Hare and planned by Spalding and Cross.*

Table of contents

Introduction 5

Boundaries and beginnings 6

1 Changes in land ownership and use, 1500-1685 7
An entertaining rural idyll
Urbane and genteel Hoxton
Dissenting Hoxton

2 Charitable and social provision, 1660-1863 13
Almshouses
Asylums, workhouses and hospitals and poverty in the East End

3 The nineteenth century 20
Population growth and housing in Hoxton
Ministering to the new population
School building
Public facilities
Penny gaffs, music halls and theatres

Final thoughts on architectural conservation in Hoxton 40

Endnotes 41

Bibliography 43

Introduction

There are only a few buildings left in Hoxton to tell its long and fascinating history. The survivors huddle along the spine of Hoxton Street and line the sides of Hoxton Square. A few more monuments are scattered about the parish church of St John the Baptist in the New North Road and around the former Haberdasher Aske's Hospital in Chart Street. These buildings, taken together with a handful of truncated terraces in the surrounding streets, give some idea of what the area was like in the early part of the nineteenth century when it enjoyed a brief spell as a bustling middle-class suburb similar to those being developed at the same time around Islington Green and St John's at Hackney. Islington and Hackney have retained a good deal more of their buildings than Hoxton where many of the old streets have now been swept away. [*Frontispiece, figure 1*] Many of the buildings which survived the war damage fell to the urban renewal programs of the Metropolitan Borough of Shoreditch during the 1950s and 1960s. The worst slums were replaced by council housing and by Shoreditch Park. We have to imagine that when the nineteenth-century Board School in Gopsall Street (now the Whitmore School) was first opened it towered above dingy, overcrowded houses and dank, airless streets, a symbol of progressive social policies pursued at local and national levels. Although it is now marooned in a vast expanse of green, the Whitmore School still functions as a focal point in a public improvement scheme, albeit one of a very different kind. The combination of council housing and large turfed spaces punctuated by the odd Victorian building or two can be found throughout the East End, and, indeed, in any part of London where local authorities tried to remake decayed and impoverished townscapes to the benefit of local people.

This book attempts to fill in the history of such gaps left by post-war planning in order to give back Hoxton some small part of the rich history which is now only glimpsed in archival sources. The first section examines land use and ownership in Hoxton from the time of the Tudors to the early eighteenth century, demonstrating how two features of Hoxton's early history exerted a tremendous influence on its later development.

First, the division of the land into small landholdings, which prevented the sort of development which made the West End of London a desirable and prosperous area; and, second, the very proximity of Hoxton to the City. Just outside the medieval walls, Hoxton was ideally placed to receive refugees. Activities which the City Aldermen banished and institutions which could not find a home in the crowded streets of the City thrived in Hoxton's green and less expensive precincts. By the start of the seventeenth century Hoxton had a slightly rough character with an exceptionally high concentration of poor people. The few pockets of gentility were gradually overwhelmed, and then obliterated by the middle of the nineteenth century. In Charles Booth's monumental study published in 1889-90, *Life and Labour of the People of London*, Shoreditch appears as one of the most deprived areas of the Metropolis. Booth identified the vast majority of streets in the western half of Hoxton as 'Poor' or 'Very Poor' and Hoxton Market was characterised as crime ridden and pestilential.

The second and third sections of this essay examine the institutions and initiatives which grew up in response to this deprivation. By 1700 there was a very high concentration of almshouses in Shoreditch parish, of which Hoxton was part, and by the end of the century, several well-known asylums had been established in Hoxton which became synonymous with Bedlam as the place where the mentally ill or incapacitated were sent for such treatment and care as there was. In 1780, the large parish workhouse opened at the north end of Hoxton, filling most of the entire block bounded by Kingsland Road, Hoxton Street and Nuttall Street. The catchment area for these institutions, particularly the workhouse, was large. Inmates came from parts of London which were already built up and where property was too valuable to be given over to such institutions. The almshouses, asylums and workhouse cast a blight on Hoxton, explaining in large part why the gentility to be found in other near suburbs such as Islington never took root in Hoxton. The horrible tenements described by Booth and immortalised by Arthur Morrison in *A Child of the Jago* (set just over Kingsland Road in Haggerston) were the result of these historical circumstances.

1 *Frontispiece. Ordnance Survey Map. Hoxton, 1871.*

Boundaries and beginnings

From the late fifteenth through early nineteenth centuries, Hoxton was more or less confined to the area between Hoxton Street and Kingsland Road, the chief Roman Road leading north out of the City. The location of Hoxton Street just beside and almost exactly parallel to this ancient road suggests that it might have started as a kind of rural lane running along the rear verge of medieval strip fields. Manmade features have always had more to do with Hoxton's history than its natural geography, which was unremarkable. The cutting of the City Road in 1761, allowing traffic to pass along Old Street to Islington, and the opening the Grand Union Canal in 1814 helped shape the area we know today, giving it distinct south and north boundaries and, more importantly, the beginnings of an economic and transport infrastructure. Shepherdess Walk, a garden path dating to the early eighteenth century, forms the western edge of the district and of the old parish of St Leonard's Shoreditch, of which Hoxton was part. The name Hoxton (the exact derivation of which has been a matter of debate since the sixteenth century) was extended over this whole area in 1829 when the ecclesiastical districts of Haggerston and Hoxton were carved out of St Leonard's parish to minister more effectively to a growing population.[1]

1
CHANGES IN LANDOWNERSHIP AND USE, 1500-1685

AN ENTERTAINING RURAL IDYLL

In medieval times Hoxton was mostly divided into small landholdings. At the very north, now bisected by the Canal, was Hoxton Manor itself, an estate of some 130 acres transferred from the parish of Hackney to Shoreditch in 1666. There was a small hamlet clustering around St Leonard's Church and another at the north end of Hoxton Street. Over the course of the sixteenth century the settlements at the north and south ends of Hoxton Street gradually expanded as London itself was being pushed outside the boundaries of its medieval walls by an increase in international trade. In 1568 the Portuguese ambassador built a fine detached house at the south end of Hoxton to escape the crowded conditions in the City and in the 1570s several foreign merchant families did likewise. Many of the foreign residents were Nonconformists (the term usually applied to Protestants who do not conform to the doctrines of the Church of England) or Roman Catholics, a fact which helped to establish Hoxton as a centre of religious dissent in London.[2] The two halves of Hoxton remained quite separate, that to the north having a rural character well into the eighteenth century. A plan of it drawn up in 1764 (*figure 2*) shows one estate belonging to Hugh Phillips, whose house was made from timber and surrounded by small outbuildings to form courtyards, an arrangement which may well have dated to the fourteenth or fifteenth centuries. Nearby was the house of Thomas Benn, built from a material first introduced on a large scale in the Tudor period, brick.[3]

This promising start to development had been slowed by a Royal Proclamation of 1580. Elizabeth I ordered that no new residences were to be constructed within three miles of the City Gates. James I issued similar bans. The effect of these proclamations was to leave Hoxton in a kind of Green Belt. As late as 1780 Hoxton was a supplier of fresh food to the City and a place of small gardens.[4] Of greater importance for the future of the area was the Lord Mayor of London's decision in 1575 to ban all theatrical performances within the City Walls. James Burbage, an actor who lived in Shoreditch, decided to take advantage of the ban by building a theatre just outside the City. In 1576 he leased land near the corner of Great Eastern Street and New Inn Yard, and converted a large barn on the site to his first venue, which was called simply 'The Theatre' and which seated six hundred people. It was the first public theatre in London and one of the earliest in Europe. Burbage's business continued growing and in 1577-8 he built a second venue, The Curtain, south of Holywell Lane. The lease on 'The Theatre' came to an end in 1598. Its timbers are said to have been reused to build the Globe Theatre on Bankside. The Curtain continued to stage performances until 1625, when the City compelled all theatres to move across the river to Southwark.[5] (See Chapter 4 for later developments.)

Many of the residents enticed outside the City walls to attend theatricals ventured a little further north to practice archery and visit alehouses in the fields west of Hoxton Street. By the 1590s Pimlico Pleasure Gardens were established on the west side of Hoxton Street, in the vicinity of Bacchus Walk. They were named after a previous tenant on the property. (Pimlico in Victoria came later.) In addition to archery fields and ale houses,

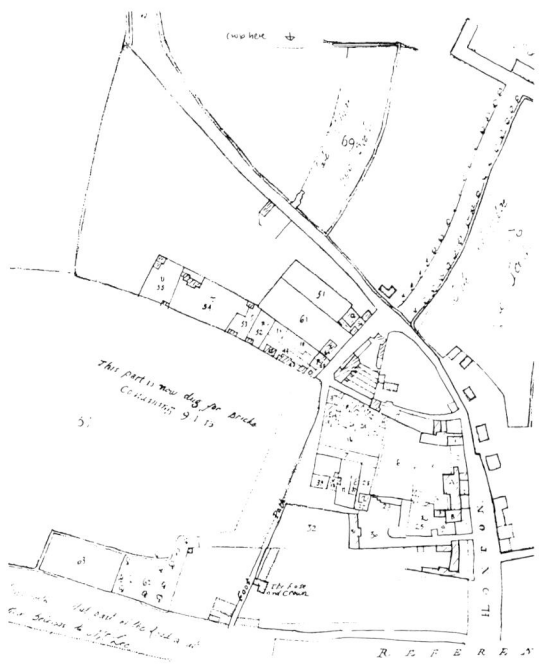

2 *Plan of the Hamlet of Hoxton, 1764.*

[7]

3   *St. John's House, Hoxton Street, c1610.*

there were prostitutes, leading one mid seventeenth-century commentator to call Hoxton a 'mistrusted locality'. A freeman barber set up there to treat syphilis and related conditions in 1641.[6]

These activities went on right next to the residences of the Hoxton's wealthy inhabitants. One of the grandest of these late Tudor and Stuart houses is recorded in a late eighteenth-century engraving, a house reputedly built in 1610 by the relatives of Lord St John, Baron of Bletsoe, whose family is buried at St Leonard's [*figure 3*]. The use of classical pilasters, stacked one upon the other, the broken segmental pediment over the entrance, the classically-styled door case, and the form of the second-floor windows are consistent with a building of this date, and the air of decay which hangs about the house in this late eighteenth-century engraving is consistent with its later history. In 1740 it was converted into a boarding school and in 1750 it became a workhouse for the poor and indigent from several City parishes. In the late eighteenth century, one of the rooms was used as a Methodist meeting hall, the Bethesda Chapel. The house was pulled down after 1845 and several houses erected on the site in a new street called Henry Place.[7]

The grandest structure in Hoxton was Balmes House, located just north of the Grand Union Canal on line with present day Whitmore Road [*figure 4*]. Balmes House was built as a grand country seat in about 1635 on the foundations of a twelfth-century manor house. (The name derived from a former owner, Adam Bamme, who was Lord Mayor of London in 1390.) Sir George Whitmore, Master of the Haberdashers' Company and Lord Mayor of London, bought the original house and its 130 acre estate in 1634. The work was probably finished by November of 1641, when Whitmore received Charles I at Balmes.

The compact rectangular plan, with an entrance and stair hall running through the centre of the house, and the giant doubled pilasters dividing the elevation into evenly spaced bays are features found on the most up-to-date architecture of this period.[8] There is some evidence to suggest that a late medieval house survived under this fashionable and grand skin. Several views of Balmes show a shallow, two-storey wing projecting from the east side of the house. This wing may have been part of a medieval house that survived at the core of Balmes. Richard de Beauvoir then became the owner of Balmes from 1680 to his death in 1708. Afterwards it was converted into an asylum for the rich, known first as Whitmore's House and then as Warburton's,

4 *Balmes House, c1635, for Sir George Whitmore, shown here in a watercolour by Toussaint.*

after a notorious proprietor.[9] As late as 1850, the house stood, surrounded by high brick walls, in the middle of fields at the north end of Whitmore Road. By 1870, it was gone and its grounds filled with substandard working-class tenements.[10]

URBANE AND GENTEEL HOXTON, 1660-1700

After a flurry of building projects executed during the reigns of the Tudor and early Stuart monarchs, the development of Hoxton slowed dramatically. The construction of Balmes and the residence of a powerful landowner might have encouraged growth had any hope for continued development not been lost with the start of the Civil War in the summer of 1642. Two decades of frustrated economic growth burst forth after the Restoration of the Monarchy in 1660. Life outside the fortified City walls was made more attractive by the return of stability and by the plague of 1665 which struck down many City dwellers. The Great Fire of 1666 then drove people to the near suburbs. Many never returned.[11] Enterprising landlords with large estates in the West End realised that the fear of conditions in the City made their lands more attractive and profitable. There followed a speculative building boom of unprecedented proportions, one which would bring a measure of urbanity to Hoxton.

The idea to develop the suburbs with luxurious residences arranged in neat geometrical ranges around planted squares was first hatched decades before the Fire. The building of Great Queen Street, Lincoln's Inn Fields and Covent Garden in the 1620s and 1630s set an important precedent. When stability returned under Charles II, the time for genteel squares lined with classically proportioned houses was right. Lord Southampton's Bloomsbury Square development of 1661 was a great success and was followed by St James's Square begun in 1665, Leicester Square in 1670 and Soho Square in 1681, to name only a few. The pattern for the development of each was roughly similar. First, a landowner laid out the estate and granted building leases. Sometimes the landowners would lease to a developer who would then lease the land in small plots to builders. The leases charged a peppercorn for the first few years while the builder raised the houses and also stipulated the materials and dimensions of the structures to be erected. Builders were often required to submit their work to inspection by an estate surveyor so that the units would conform to a type and produce a pleasing, unified whole. The standardization of types allowed the landowner and developer to set rents and calculate likely revenues.

The landowner or developer usually took the lead in establishing the district as a genteel and fashionable quarter by building a grand house for himself in the square. Those estates planned with the greatest care included a market for the future tenants and less expensive streets for tradesmen. The centres of the squares were left open to serve as small parks for the residents and to relieve the urban congestion which had encouraged the spread of disease and fire.[12]

Hoxton Square was developed in part along these lines. The land at the south end of Hoxton Street was owned by the Austen family who leased it in 1683 it to two developers, Samuel Blewitt and Robert Hacksaw. The developers relet the land in small lots to builders. The square was completed by the 1720s.[13] The exterior walls of the new townhouses were made from brick and their roofs were covered in tile or slate. Building regulations passed after the Great Fire required the use of fire resistant materials. Most of the houses were two storeys tall with a basement, and roof dormers lighting the servants' quarters. The residences in Hoxton Square were smaller than their West End contemporaries, which tended to have three or four storeys and, in a few cases, architecturally grand touches. The most characteristic feature of this new generation of townhouse was the sash window, which had gradually replaced casement windows from the middle of the seventeenth century.

Surveying Hoxton Square today it is hard to imagine it built up with neat, two-storey brick houses. Most of the structures date from the late nineteenth or early twentieth centuries; they are larger than the seventeenth-century houses which once lined the square and built to serve different functions. However the feeling of an enclosed square persists. The east side retains something of the original scale of the development. Nos. 31 and 37 were refronted in the nineteenth century. No. 32 has recently been restored to an original design [*Figure* 5]. The purple-brown brick of the front wall appears to be completely new, a skin covering original wall (notice how the brick projects nearly one brick beyond the surface of the adjacent structure), although the pattern of the bricks, laid in what is known as Flemish bond, is as one would expect in buildings of this date.

Hoxton's proximity to the City made it a desirable location and a second development was soon begun. In the spring of 1684 William Charles leased a plot of land in the north-east corner of a square just being laid out to the west of Hoxton Square. For a time it was identified only as New Square, but it eventually came to be called after its first resident. The east side of Charles Square was completed in 1685 but the north and west sides were only partly developed by the time of Peter Chassereau's 1745 *Survey of Shoreditch* [*figure* 6]. The south side remained a garden to the 1770s. The houses of Charles Square were built from the same range of materials as those used in Hoxton Square but on a somewhat grander scale. The only one to survive is No. 16 [*figure* 7] a mid eighteenth-century structure which served as the County Court during the nineteenth century and is now used by the Labour Party as Regional Offices. It is shocking to think that many beautiful houses with fine panelled rooms and carved doorcases survived until the 1950s, only to be demolished.

The developers of Hoxton and Charles Squares counted on Hoxton Street to provide the necessary services for their elegant new squares and left the provision of a market area to speculative development and chance. Not long after the laying out of Charles Square, Messrs Ball

5 *No. 32 Hoxton Square, late seventeenth century. Photo Author.*

[10]

and Brown took out long leases on the land between the two Squares from Sir Charles Pitfield. On 17 January of 1687 or 1688, the developers obtained a licence to hold a market on the site on Tuesdays and Saturdays, one day for meat and the other for produce. The venture was a spectacular and almost immediate failure.[14] In *A Tour through London about the Year 1725*, Daniel Defoe noted that the streets around the two Squares were 'all open fields', including the site 'intended for a marketplace', which he described as forlorn.[15]

DISSENTING HOXTON

Hoxton Square quickly developed a character quite different from any other London Square. By the close of the seventeenth century it was renowned as a hotbed of Nonconformity. Even before Blewitt and Hacksaw leased the land, the Rev. Thomas Vincent, who had been ejected from the Church of England in 1666, gathered an independent congregation around him at the south end of Hoxton Street. Several members of this congregation stayed behind after Vincent's chapel moved to Hand Alley in Bishopsgate in 1678, and in 1699 the well known Dissenting Academy of Coventry relocated to Hoxton Square, attracted not only by Vincent's early success and the presence of his followers, but also by the area's cosmopolitan character.[16] A London location was thought to be essential in order to obtain a higher quality of tutor and student. The appointment of Jacques Cappel (1639-1722), a French refugee who had taught Hebrew at the University of Saumur, to the faculty in 1708 established Hoxton Academy as a school of the highest rank.[17]

The Academy tutors tended to live in the Square itself or in Hoxton Street, giving the south end of the Hoxton an almost collegiate air. Some twenty five Nonconformist ministers in all lived in the Square over the course of the eighteenth century. The Academy's most famous student was William Godwin, the noted political radical and intellectual, who attended from 1773 to 1778. It was here that Godwin met Mary Wollstonecraft who lived nearby.

In 1785 the first Hoxton Academy closed. Its chief tutors, Andrew Kippis (1725-95, a noted antiquarian and a Fellow of the Society of Antiquaries) and Abraham Rees (1743-1825) took up chairs at Homerton College on Homerton High Street which had been founded as a Dissenters' Academy in 1769. The intellectual approach of the first Hoxton Academy was out of step with changes in Nonconformist thinking. Its maintenance grant, paid out of the Congrega-tional Fund, was terminated. Nonconformity was starting to develop a strong evangelical emphasis and Evangelical Christianity was soon seen in Hoxton. In 1784 a Dissenting Academy, also called Hoxton Academy, was founded in the Square on the new evangelical principles. It came to include a Sunday School and Chapel and

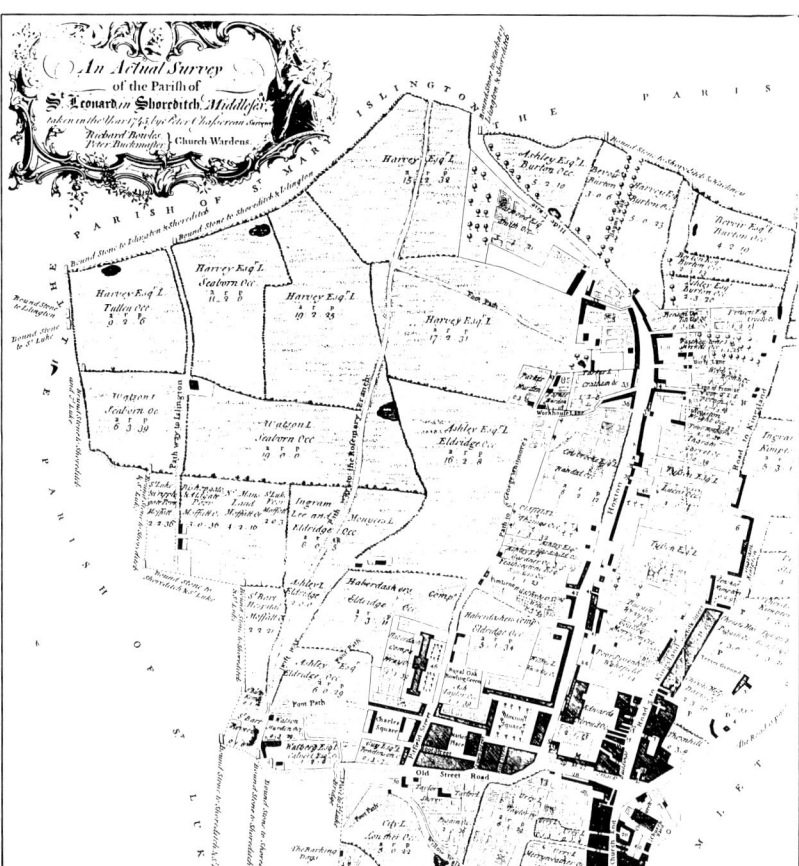

6 (above) *Detail from Chassereau's 'Survey of Shoreditch', 1745.*

7 *No. 16, Charles Square, early eighteenth century. Photo Author.*

8   *The second Hoxton Academy, Hoxton Street, 1814, shown here in a late nineteenth-century view.*

9   *Proposed refronting of the Hoxton Academy, Hoxton Street, 1855. Never carried out.*

10   *Reeves Place Methodist Church, 1789.*

moved into specially built premises in 1814, at no. 93 Hoxton Street [*figure 8*]. In 1855 the Academy tried to raise funds for a program of expansion which included refronting the old structure in a skin of stucco cement pressed into Italian Renaissance forms [*figure 9*]. The campaign failed and the early nineteenth-century building stood until war damage forced its demolition.

Of considerably more architectural interest was the first Methodist Church in Hoxton, built on the corner of Hoxton Street and Reeves Place, near present-day Wilmer Gardens [*figure 10*]. Two storeys tall, its main front was faced in cream coloured stucco, which was just then coming into vogue, and divided into three bays by round-arched recesses. The elevation finished in a triangular pediment. The two tiers of windows, which returned to Reeves Place, indicate that the interior was planned for galleries on three sides, an arrangement which was typical of Methodist Churches.

In the early eighteenth century, Hoxton was also home to a small Jewish community, no more than the fringe of much larger communities in Spitalfields, Bethnal Green and Shoreditch. Since 1650 Jewish settlement had concentrated on the east side of the City. Because of the Orthodox prohibition against travelling on the Sabbath or on Holydays, these communities remained in the East End to stay within easy walking distance of their synagogues. The Shoreditch community was concentrated around St Leonard's Church and Hoxton Street and by the early eighteenth century, it had established a burial ground at the south end of Hoxton Street, along its east side. It was closed to burials in 1799 and later partly built over by the Hoxton House Asylum. An LCC school of the early twentieth century now stands on the site. Middle class Jews left the area between 1825 and 1850 for Whitechapel and Mile End, where the tradition of Jewish settlement continued to make the East End the first port of call for the huge numbers of Jewish immigrants who arrived between 1870 to 1914.[18]

2
CHARITABLE AND SOCIAL PROVISION, 1660-1863

ALMSHOUSES

While Hoxton might not have been swallowed up in a speculative housing boom, it was soon thickly populated by almoners living in almshouses established by special charities, trusts or churches for people who were poor, infirm or widowed. The growth in private wealth during the Tudor and Stuart periods, in addition to Thomas Cranmer's call for faithful Anglicans to divert funds formerly given to monasteries and chantry endowments to the poor, brought about a boom in almshouse building during the seventeenth and eighteenth centuries. Although ostensibly charitable institutions, every group of almshouses had a donor's plaque or even a life-size statue of the founder in a prominent location recording his or her generosity.[19]

The south border of Hoxton was known for its dense concentration of almshouses. Peter Chassereau's 1745 Survey of the parish lists close to twenty in the whole parish [*see figure 6 above*]. The first to be endowed was Fuller's Hospital, located on the south side of Old Street, on the site of Shoreditch Town Hall. In a will dated 29 March 1592, John Fuller of Stepney, who was a judge in the reign of Elizabeth, directed his wife to erect two 'hospitals of almshouses', one in Stepney for twelve men, and the other in Shoreditch for twelve women. The almoners had to be at least fifty years old. Each received an annual stipend generated by farmlands in Lincolnshire. Construction was delayed for close to a century while sufficient funds accumulated from land revenues and it was not until 1687 that eight aldermen of the Mercers' Company, who had been charged with administering the charitable part of Fuller's estate, commissioned almshouses with a frontage of 165 feet along Old Street [*figure 11*]. The group shown in this late eighteenth-century watercolour has been dated to 1787, when the dilapidated row was rebuilt with funds raised by voluntary subscription in the parish. Maintenance of the almshouses passed to the Parish Poor Trustees in the early nineteenth century.[20]

The earliest Hoxton almshouses to be built were those endowed in 1658 by John Walter, a member of the Drapers' Company who left funds for the care of 'some of the many poor, aged and distressed people' in the parish of Shoreditch.[21] A low terrace of eight houses, one for each almoner, was put up on the north side of Old Street near the corner with Kingsland Road. After the death of Walter's widow, the Company of Drapers accepted management of the almshouses and took the opportunity to reserve two places in the group for the widows of deceased members of the Drapers'. Their manner of selecting almoners was typical and is recorded in an 1836 review of charitable provision in the Parish of Shoreditch. When a space became vacant, the Churchwarden of St Leonard's called a public meeting, usually on a Sunday after the evening sermon. Women in the parish who were of 'good name' and in need were elected before the parish Vestry. In general the poorest was chosen. If any member of the Company of Drapers or a Churchwarden objected, then the election was held again. Every month the minister or someone in his charge visited each almoner. If any one had a special problem then the parish could appeal to the Company of Drapers to meet the cost. All almoners had special seats in St Leonard's and were buried at the cost of the parish in the churchyard. Not all, however, received the same benefits. The places in the gift of the Drapers paid

11 *Fuller's Almshouses, Old Street. Established in a will dated 1592. View by Shepherd of the group as rebuilt in 1787.*

[13]

higher stipends and gave the inmates more fuel in the winter than those endowed by Mr Walter. The whole group became dilapidated and was rebuilt on a larger scale in 1826 for a total of eighteen inmates. Eight of the new places were endowed by one of the Parish's Poor Trustees, Mr Thomas Porter, who levied and managed the parish poor rate. The remaining units were paid for and endowed by public subscription.[22] The management of the group passed to the Parish of St Leonard's from this point. All the parish poor, aged and infirm came under the authority of the Poor Trustees following the 1723 Workhouse Act. To meet their statutory obligations, the Trustees levied a poor rate, based on the rental value of the property. The rate varied from parish to parish and annually depending on need.

The number of almshouses in Hoxton grew quickly in the last third of the seventeenth century, leaving the parish of Shoreditch with more almshouses than any other adjoining parish in the orbit of the City. In 1669, on a site immediately to the west of Walter's Almshouses, the Weavers' Company erected a range of almshouses for twelve widows of their company who were elected by a special Court of Assistants. The Weaver's almshouses were rebuilt on a larger scale in the same year as Walter's. To the rear was a set of houses built from funds left by Daniel Badger of Haggerston in a will dated 7 February, 1674. The site was purchased in 1694 and six almshouses built in two equal ranges which faced onto a narrow courtyard entered from Hoxton Street. Badger left no funds for an endowment to pay benefits to the almoners who were supported out of the parish poor rates.[23] One of the last groups in Shoreditch was built in 1734, the Framework Knitters' Almshouses, twelve cottages arranged on three sides of a square planted with a garden. The only survival of this entire generation of building is the group built by Sir Robert Geffrye in 1715 and managed by the Ironmongers' Company, now the Geffrye Museum.

Almshouses were built in this area, at the intersection of Old Street and Kingsland Road, in order to be close to the seat of local government, the church Vestry. Although the management of each group was vested in a different City Company or trust, the Parish Vestry and later St Leonard's Poor Trustees were charged with overseeing the almoners. Indeed, the Poor Trustees could exercise control over all those in need of parish provision. With this duty, incidentally, came the power to prevent the paupers resident in other parishes from settling in Shoreditch parish. The vicar of St Leonard's took an interest in the welfare of the residents and the state of the buildings. By the start of the Victorian period, St Leonard's Vestry and Poor Trustees had assumed control of almost every almshouse in Shoreditch. Those almshouses built far from St Leonard's were administered by other churches or by independent institutions. For example, Lumley's Almshouses, established in 1672 near the bottom of Shepherdess Walk, some distance from the group of Kingsland Road/Old Street almshouses, were in the joint control of St Botolph, Bishopsgate and St Botolph, Aldgate. Since the cost of land in these City parishes was high, a site outside the City walls had to be found. A site in Shoreditch owned by the Bishopsgate parish was given for the construction of the almshouses, which were rebuilt in 1822 and demolished in 1898 after the almoners were moved to a more salubrious location.[24]

The Nonconformists of Hoxton Square were responsible for the building and maintenance of almshouses on a smaller scale than the Anglicans, in keeping with their more modest means. The first gift was made by William Berman, a Nonconformist minister who lived in Hoxton Square. His will of 1700 directed executors to purchase some estate in houses or in land for a trust to fund almshouses. In 1704 a strip of land on Kingsland Road was purchased. The rent charged was used to build and maintain the almshouses which were located at the rear of Basing Place, a small court of terraced houses about 500 feet from the east end of Old Street and entered from Kingsland Road. In 1707, the garden on the west verge of the site was let for use as the Jewish Burial Ground mentioned earlier. The rest of the site was let to Hoxton House Elementary School. In 1784, the entire western half of the Berman's Trust Estate, as well as property to the north and south belonging to Sir Jonathan Miles, was united to form Hoxton House Lunatic Asylum. Four more Nonconformist almshouses were endowed and built over the next century. In 1749 Mary Westby of Bocking in Essex bought a site south of Bacchus Walk on the line of what is now Pitfield Street. She ordered that three inmates be selected from each of three sects, the Independents, the Presbyterians and the 'Antipaedo Baptists'. In the 1810s a Presbyterian Mr Fuller, who had been a banker in Lombard Street in the City, endowed places for nine Presbyterian women in the newly cut Gloucester Street, north of Pimlico and south of present-day Bacchus Walk. A second Fuller's Almshouse was built in Hoxton Old Town, and a third opposite the Hoxton House Asylum on Hoxton Street. By 1811 an almshouse for four widows who were members of the Trinity Street Chapel was built in Phillipp Street. In the same year a Wesleyan Congregation built a small group in Reeves Place.[25]

12 *The first Aske's Almshouses and Schools, Chart Street, designed by Robert Hooke, 1690-95.*

All the Hoxton almshouses were built in a modest style with the exception of one, Haberdasher's Aske's Almshouses and Schools, which was architecture on a grand scale and remained the only charitable institution with monumental intentions until the Victorian period [*figure 12*]. Its history began in the ordinary way. In a bequest of 1689 Robert Aske, a member of the Haberdashers' Company, gave funds to build a hospital for 20 poor men and women associated with the Company. What made Aske's gift unusual was the amount, close to £24,000, a huge sum in those days, and the condition that the Company also maintain and educate twenty sons of poor freemen. The Charity incorporated in 1690 to carry out his intentions purchased 21 acres of land in Hoxton and 2,000 acres of land in Kent, generating an annual income of £765. The cost of these investments had been £13,211, leaving some £11,000 to spend on constructing the Hospital and School building which went up to the west of Pitfield Street. The building budget was large enough to provide a grand and fine structure designed by an architect, Dr Robert Hooke, who had worked as a scientist and physician before the Great Fire. He impressed the City Common Council with plans for the rebuilding of London after the Fire and in recognition of his skill they appointed him one of the surveyors charged with overseeing the rebuilding. A close friend and associate of Wren, whom he assisted on some of the City Churches, Hooke's best known building was Bethlehem Hospital in Moorgate of 1675.

Hooke's Aske's Hospital was organised on a pavilion plan, with end units tied to a pedimented centre section by low wings fronted by a loggia. The inmates lived in the wings. The common areas, school rooms and chapel, were set in the centre. The Chaplain's apartments were in the two-storey end block to the north and the boys sleeping quarters in an identical structure to the south; to the rear was a playground. The design is more complex than it at first appears; especially curious is the feeling of mass hovering over void and the odd changes in window rhythym and scale. Hooke's great work had grown dilapidated and out of fashion by the early nineteenth century, and in 1825 David Riddel Roper was commissioned to rebuild it. Roper's building was completed in 1827 and is the one we see today. Like Hooke's work, Roper's is organised on a pavilion plan, with pedimented centre and projecting end wings, but here the similarity ends

13 *Early nineteenth-century engraving of the new Aske's Almshouses and Schools, as built to the designs of David Riddel Roper and completed in 1827.*

14 *No.237 Hoxton Street. Artisan's dwelling of c1700. Currently in the process of restoration by Julian Harrap Architects. Photo Author.*

15 *No.47 Charles Square. Artisan's cottage of early to mid eighteenth century, with some nineteenth-century alterations. Photo Author.*

[*figure 13*]. Where Hooke's design seemed about to lift from the ground on thin legs, Roper's is firmly planted on it, weighed down by a primitive Greek Doric portico. The wall openings are regular and even, punctures in the bare unrelieved walls of plain London stock brick. The movement in the elevation is stopped dead by the stout corner piers of the end bays. Aske's Hospital was extended in a sympathetic style during an 1873 conversion into a National School. In 1898, the boys were moved to a school in West Hampstead and the girls to one in Acton, and the London County Council took over the building for use as Shoreditch Technical College in the early twentieth century.[26]

This survey has concentrated on the houses of the wealthy and structures built by donation for the care of the area's poor, sick and aged. How and where did most people in Hoxton live? Some of the poorest people lived in makeshift shacks thrown together from a variety of materials. Others lived in tenements. People who practised a skilled trade had a better standard of living and could afford houses built from longer lasting and more weathertight materials. Hoxton is fortunate to have a rare survival of this type, no. 237 Hoxton Street, of 1700-1730 [*figure 14*]. The original character of the building is almost completely obscured by late Victorian shop fronts; above one can just make out the brickwork characteristic of the early Georgian period and which has recently been cleaned as part of a scheme of conservation being carried out by Julian Harrap Architects. The tile covered roof, eaves cornice and hipped dormers have recently been renewed.[27] Nos.124 and 126 date from the same time but built on a somewhat grander scale. Nos.173 and 175 were built sometime in the first half of the eighteenth century, refronted around 1800 and harshly restored in recent times. Further north, on the east side, stood a group of similar houses which were demolished in the early 1970s.[28] Although the buildings which line Hoxton Street appear for the most part to date to the mid nineteenth century, the "jogging" line of building fronts records a late seventeenth-century or possibly even earlier settlement pattern. There may even be several very old buildings or foundations waiting to be discovered beneath relatively modern fronts. Another rare survival of an early tradesman's house stands at the south entrance to Charles Square, no.47 [*figure 15*]. Although the windows appear to have been altered in the early nineteenth century, the low floor heights, silhouette and overall scale of the building, as well as its position at the mouth of a mid eighteenth-century square, suggest a date of 1770 or slightly earlier.

ASYLUMS, WORKHOUSES, HOSPITALS AND POVERTY IN THE EAST END

Apart from a few projects, such as the construction of tenements between 1718 and 1735 in Pitfield Street, Hoxton remained a largely agricultural district through most of the eighteenth century.[29] Agricultural improvements over the course of the century and the progress of enclosures and drainage schemes made farming a profitable venture, with the greatest revenues coming generally between 1760 and 1790. As late as 1800, the cultivated countryside encroached on the borders of the growing metropolis, bringing city and country hard up against one another.

Because of its position on the verge of London, isolated in farmland and yet close to main thoroughfares, Hoxton was an ideal place for asylums caring for the mentally ill and disabled. For most of the eighteenth century, Hoxton was synonymous with Bedlam, as the the Royal Bethlehem Hospital, then in Moorfields, was called.[30] Three asylums opened in Hoxton during the eighteenth century: Warburton's, Holly House and Hoxton House. Despite the high fees charged by Warburton's, located in Balmes House, the Parliamentary Select Committee which investigated the care of the mentally ill and disabled from 1815 to 1819 found conditions there appalling and recommended urgent reforms. Holly House, located on the east side of Hoxton Street, was a small institution run on more humane principles; the noted physician James Parkinson, who lived at no.1 Hoxton Square, was its medical attendant during the early nineteenth century.

The largest asylum was Hoxton House, founded in 1695 on the east side of Hoxton Street just north of Hoxton Square. In 1784 the owner of the asylum, Sir Jonathan Miles purchased a large plot of land from Berman's Trust to enlarge the premises by building ward blocks separated only by narrow alleys and courts. The expanded asylum, which stood to the north of the Jewish Burial Ground, attracted patients from all over London. The buildings were enlarged once again in 1814, at which point Hoxton House had 484 patients.[31] Although the Parliamentary Select Committee criticised its crowded conditions, the number of inmates decreased very slowly. By 1849 there were still over 400 patients. 39 men and 74 women were private patients. The fees of the remaining 122 men and 196 women were paid by the Poor Trustees of several parishes.[32] In the late nineteenth century, the London School Board took over the site which then passed to the London County Council. It is now covered with a collection of mainly Victorian brick school buildings which, oddly enough, give some sense of the scale of the old asylum buildings.

At the same time that Hoxton House Asylum was expanding, the first parish workhouse was established near Nuttall Street on a parcel of land which had been known as 'Land of Promise' since the sixteenth century. In 1774 an Act of Parliament authorised the Shoreditch Vestry to levy a special poor rate for the construction of a workhouse. The parish finances were being strained by the increase in the number of poor and indigent people who were boarded in private poorhouses at the parish's expense. Because these private 'Farmed Houses' were independent of any regulation, conditions varied considerably.

In 1776, the 'Land of Promise' site was given to the Parish Poor Trustees who let the western part to generate income.[33] The new St Leonard's workhouse was completed in 1777. Its principal front faced Kingsland Road. The brick building was three storeys high and articulated into three bays which projected slightly and were capped by shallow pediments. Otherwise there was very little to relieve its high sheer bulk.[34] In 1784 the Bishop of London consecrated a burial ground for inmates in the southwest corner of the site. Nearby was a garden and recreation yard.[35] The new workhouse had a small infirmary and apothecary which were not concessions to charity or public health but safeguards to the investment of the parish ratepayers. The Poor Trustees sold the labour of inmates to private businesses to recover money spent on building and maintaining the institution. Although St Leonard's workhouse was constructed out of the parish poor rates, it was not run at any cost to the ratepayers. The only other health care for the poor was available in charitable hospitals where places were in the gift of wealthy patrons.[36] The vicious outbreaks of typhoid in 1819 and cholera in 1831 strained these meager public health care provisions. Although the tales of suffering in East End slums shocked the upper and middle classes, government was slow to respond.

The expiration of leases on the remaining Land of Promise lots in 1847 and the recommendations of a Special Parliamentary Subcommittee on workhouse provision which were published in the following year goaded the Poor Trustees of St Leonard's to act. The Parliamentary report found St Leonard's Workhouse overcrowded with more than 1000 inmates in a facility designed to hold a maximum of 800. 150 of these inmates were chronically ill and housed in poorly ventilated wards which were not separated from those of the healthy inmates. A separate hospital with a pure water supply was recommended.[37] Out of the great epidemics of the early part of the century came the realisation that contaminated air and water spread disease. In 1849 the Parish Poor Trustees set about rebuilding and modernising the workhouse. New blocks were built around two open courtyards. A kitchen and bakehouse were added to the rear – the first structure had neither. A special fever hospital and an infirmary

16 *St Leonard's Offices for the Relief of the Poor, designed by Lee and completed in 1863. Photo Author.*

ward were established in a separate wing. In 1850 an artesian well was completed to reduce the risk of water-bourne infections taking hold among the Workhouse inmates.

The next wave of improvement followed from the passage of the Metropolitan Management Act which, among other things, created Parish Health Officers. The first Health Officer of Shoreditch, a Dr Barnes, published a detailed account of the state of the parish in 1858. The conditions he reported were appalling. It was clear that the improvement of conditions inside the Workhouse made little difference to those outside. Infant mortality in the parish was over 46%, 10% higher than in the City of London which had been pursuing public health measures for some time. A quarter of all deaths in 1855 were the result of typhoid, smallpox and other epidemics. The area's water supply was foul and the drainage system almost non-existent. A large percentage of the housing stock put up since 1800 was of the poorest quality, thrown up in small alleys and courts which were virtual sewers and without even the most basic facilities. Earlier housing built on a more generous scale had been subdivided to accommodate a higher concentration of people and so was little better. Dr Barnes did all the things which became standard operating practice for later housing and social reformers, such as cutting new windows in crowded courts, and cleansing and trapping drains. Most important of all was his call to transform the workhouse infirmary into a public health centre and hospital.[38]

In order to press much needed reforms, a special Board of Guardians for Shoreditch was created in February of 1859 under the terms of the Poor Law Board Regulations. One of its first acts was to add committee rooms and offices to the old workhouse so that they could carry out their work more effectively.[39] In 1861 the Guardians formed a Building Committee to oversee the construction of a new workhouse and infirmary for 1200 people and which would include a health centre to the Hoxton Steet elevation. By February of 1863 a tender for £40,000 submitted by Perry and Co, builders of Stratford, was accepted; the architect was a Mr Lee, with offices in Cornhill. The funds were borrowed from the Public Works Loan Committee, who brokered public loans. The mortgage was held by the Metropolitan Life Assurance Company.[40]

The St Leonard's Offices for Relief of the Poor was completed by the autumn of 1863 [*figure 16*] and the workhouse not long afterwards.[41] The workhouse and infirmary blocks are typical of their kind: the elevations are long, unrelenting and utilitarian in character with a minimum of architectural embellishment. The sheer bulk of the block is impressive if a little grim, a testament to the strict economies imposed on public provision. What little money was left over in the budget for decoration, the architect expended on the Poor Relief Offices which face Hoxton Street. Here the brown brick of the workhouse gives way to red brick and stone dressings; the pediment on the first floor has a carving in high relief of a lion rampant. Although this elevation is by no means

[18]

17 *St Leonard's Workhouse and Infirmary, Nuttall Street elevation. Designed by Lee, and erected c.1865. Photo Author.*

grand, the design is handsome. The Board of Guardians clearly wanted the Poor Relief Offices to stand as a gesture of munificence, although it has to be said that this gesture was too late and too little to relieve the suffering of the residents of Hoxton.[42]

Today the buildings on the site are empty and the subject of redevelopment proposals. The workhouse is likely to be demolished, the Poor Relief Offices to remain. The removal of the workhouse, in particular that wing which abuts the Poor Relief Offices, would be an historical loss. The Poor Relief Offices are valuable and interesting in part because of their very difference from the workhouse. The collision of styles along Hoxton Street, the very awkwardness of the join between the Offices and the end pavilion of of the workhouse, is a graphic reminder of the painful emergence of public health care facilities from the workhouse. The long elevation of the workhouse [*figure 17*] also sets the context for James Brooks' great masterpiece, the former Church of St Columba and its related buildings to the east on Kingsland Road (discussed below). The gigantic, towering scale of Brooks' design was, as architectural critics noted when construction began in 1869, conceived in response to the enormity of the workhouse. St Columba's was built as a slum mission centre, with a cloister to the north formed by National schools and a dormitory for resident clergy. Removing the workhouse, the most tangible sign of the area's past, will rob Brooks' masterpiece, one of the greatest slum churches of the Victorian period and Listed Grade I, of its context, much as would the demolition of the elevation of St Leonard's Hospital facing Kingsland Road, completed in 1866. The combination of Poor Relief Offices, Workhouse, hospital and slum mission is not only an important monument to the beginning of the social work movement but also has important townscape value. As one moves south from Whitmore Road into Hoxton Street, the corner pavilion of the workhouse and the Poor Relief Offices are the nearest the historic street has to a gateway; cut back this corner and Hoxton Street has lost what little is left of its visual coherence. Likewise the contrast between the great, truncated tower of St Columba's and the elegant spire of St Leonard's to the south serves to mark the limit of Hoxton and Haggerston and to form another visual gateway to the East End.

3

THE NINETEENTH CENTURY: POPULATION GROWTH AND HOUSING IN NINETEENTH-CENTURY HOXTON

Even the mammoth block formed by St Leonard's Workhouse and Hospital was too small to house the mounting numbers of people who were stricken by poverty. The enormity of the problem was the result of historical changes in the late eighteenth and early nineteenth centuries. The start of the Napoleonic wars in 1793 brought about a great dock building boom which attracted thousands of skilled and unskilled labourers with their families to the City and East End. The Wars also caused a collapse in credit which bankrupted many London builders and forced dense overbuilding to very low standards simply so that builders and developers could meet the terms of their leases. The tenants who rented this substandard housing were subject to the vagaries of uncontrolled market forces. The final blow to the East End was dealt by the trade agreements with France made after Napoleonic Wars that brought about the collapse of the thriving Spitalfields silk industry. The few jobs which remained were poorly paid. Indeed, the East End has never quite recovered from the loss of this important industry.[43] In any case, the precedents for the infamous tenement courts and alleys which Booth decried in 1890 were created in the 1790s.

The process of migration and social change was swift. City dwellers who were unhappy with the noise and overcrowding caused by Dock building moved to what were then rural retreats. Islington and Hackney were favourite ports of call. Haggerston and Hoxton, which were still underdeveloped due to building restrictions imposed by Elizabeth I and James I, were also popular, but they proved only temporary refuges from the encroaching city. Working-class Dissenters in particular flocked to Hoxton because of its long history for sheltering Nonconformists.[44]

For a short time, however, the first three decades of the nineteenth century, Hoxton enjoyed life as a polite suburb. Middle-class development was concentrated around Hoxton and Charles Squares and Aske's Hospital. The first building leases in Haberdasher's Place (now Haberdasher Street) were signed in 1802. The Trustees of Aske's Hospital had hoped to develop this area to the north of the Hospital much earlier but there had simply been no demand in the previous century.[45] Development spread quickly along the spine of the New North Road (opened as a toll road in 1815) and around St John the Baptist's Church (consecrated in 1826).[46] Gloucester Street (now Crondall Street) was cut in 1815 to connect the New North Road with St John's Road (now Pitfield Street). Stimulated by the opening of the New North Road, the west side of Bridport Place was filled with houses by 1825; nos.66-80 survive with some alterations from the mid to late nineteenth century. Most important of all was the laying out of east-west streets linking Hoxton and Pitfield Streets from 1815 to 1839: Gloucester Street (Crondall Street), Myrtle Street, Ashford Street, Robert Street (demolished) and Aske Street (demolished).[47] The first houses in Ashford, Aske, Myrtle and Robert Streets went up after 1839.

Good examples of the sorts of houses put up between 1810 and 1835 can still be found in Buttesland Street, nos.60-75, Chart Street, nos. 17-23 [*figure 18*] and Pitfield Street, nos. 8 and 10. The ground floors of the latter pair were converted to shops in the late nineteenth century. Most survive in something like their original condition with only slight alterations and losses. Unfortunately, nos.31-41 New North Road, built in the 1820s, were harshly restored in the late 1980s.[48] The shops serving the new residents were located in Shoreditch High Street, well known as an elegant shopping parade during the 1820s. There were also shops located in the narrow streets leading into the old squares, such as, for example, no.56 Hoxton Square which is a more or less intact early nineteenth-century house [*figure 19*]. The ground floor was converted to a shop in the 1820s or 1830s, to judge by the style of the front. The broad sign fascia, flat modilioned cornice, and brackets flanking the entrance and on the right party wall are an original design. The shallow bowed shop window, although somewhat rebuilt in the twentieth century, is a common late Georgian or Regency type.

The forms and materials used in these terraced houses were standard and can be found on houses

18 *Nos.17-23 Chart Street. Early nineteenth-century terraced houses. Photo Author.*

19 *No.56 Hoxton Square. Early nineteenth-century house, possibly refronting of an earlier structure; shopfront of c1830. Photo Author.*

from Hackney and Islington to Peckham and Greenwich: stock brick laid in Flemish bond, stucco dressings, shallow pitched roofs hidden behind parapets, round-arched entrances with decorative fanlights, window lintels of gauged brick, elegant railings to the stairs and basement areas. Their beauty derives from the repetition of small scale elements. The resemblances between these houses and the seventeenth-century townhouses on which they were based are really only superficial. For a start, early nineteenth-century houses were more like consumer goods mass produced by a building industry than individual objects crafted by artisan labourers. From the late eighteenth century, building sites were transformed into mobile factories. The clay and gravel on a site was excavated and made into bricks and street paving. Labourers sold their work at market values, without the intervention of guilds or trade unions, to builder-contractors, who were engaged in erecting several houses at once rather than completing one before moving on to the next. Neither the rarity of surviving nineteenth-century houses – which has made them objects worthy of conservation – nor the conventional image of mass-production in permanent factory buildings should blind us to the fact that late Georgian and Victorian houses were in many ways comparable to any other factory-made item of the period. The social conditions necessary for this kind of house building were similar to those necessary for the mass production of biscuits or shoes.[49] The situation was different on some large estates, where covenants in building leases and the oversight exercised by the estate surveyor maintained high standards. There was a difference in the client group served by the first townhouses and the nineteenth-century terraces. The former were built for a restricted and wealthy clientele, the latter for a proportionally larger and less exclusive market.

Hoxton's long-term prospects for gentility, even of the mass produced variety, were not good. Besides the looming threat of disease and overcrowding creeping up from the City, Hoxton was starting to develop an industrial character. By 1799 a very large vinegar works had been built on the northeast corner of the City Road and Old Street, going right through the block to Catherine Street (now Brunswick Street). The works were a blight on the area up to the early twentieth century. The completion of the Grand Union Canal in 1814 attracted light industry and warehouses to the north border of Hoxton. Congestion increased and housing conditions rapidly worsened in the 1830s. The area's largest enterprise was the City Sawmills at the top of the New North Road. The owners, Messrs Esdailes, eventually erected several industrial dwellings for their employees, but these were little better than the squalid tenements which multiplied after 1850.

At mid century, the vicar of St John's Hoxton noted more than a dozen light industries including a dyeworks, a satindressers, engineering firms, a paper staining house and a brick yard. The latter cast a pall of smoke and filth over the surrounding district. There were also builders, cabinet makers, carpenters and hearth rug makers. The Ordnance Survey Map of 1871 [*frontispiece, figure 1*] shows small factories scattered evenly across the area, right in the midst of the closely spaced tenements. In Hoxton and Charles Squares, many of the houses survived as furniture making shops and salerooms. By the end of the nineteenth century, many small manufacturers and wholesalers needed special buildings to ply their trades and the area around Hoxton Square still contains a fair number of these structures. There are good turn of the century industrial buildings in Fanshaw Street, nos.5 and 6 (of c.1880), 8 and 9 (c.1900 and dated 1897) and no.50 Hoxton Square. A typical industrial structure of the period can be found on the corner of Coronet Street, no. 58 Hoxton Square, built in the 1890s for a firm of metal merchants and now home to the Bass Clef, a Jazz club [*figure 20*].[50]

Between 1830 and 1860, the largest undeveloped portion of Hoxton, west of Pitfield Street and stretching north to the Canal, was covered over with houses which from the outside resembled the middle class terraces of the 1820s but which were in fact built as multiple dwellings with few amenities.[51] Packed into thousands of identical dwellings were an increasing number of impoverished and working poor, the victims in part of meteoric growth in the population of Shoreditch: 53,000 inhabitants in 1821, 83,000 in 1841 and finally 129,000 recorded in the 1861 Census, the highest number of people ever to live in the parish.[52] The entire area was cleared in the decades following the Second-World War. Shoreditch Park and council housing has replaced the slum tenements.

In 1839 the second Commons Select Committee on Metropolitan Improvements published a series of recommendations to combat the growth of filthy and unhealthy slums and to ease congestion at key points in the Metropolis, including Shoreditch.[53] The Map which accompanied these proposals shows demolitions and new roads to be concentrated in Hoxton and just south of Old Street, a sure indication of the area's rapidly declining fortunes. In the event, the huge cost of the Select Committee's proposals combined with government cuts in 1840 doomed any prospect of implementing slum clearances in Shoreditch.[54]

20 *No.58 Hoxton Street. Warehouse and offices for a firm of metal merchants and dating to the 1890s. Now home to the Bass Clef Jazz Club. Photo Author.*

[22]

Although the attention of the public turned periodically to the appalling conditions in the East End during the early nineteenth century, legislation to relieve the problems was slow in coming. Following the severe winter of 1860-61, one of worst ever recorded, public and private initiatives to combat the effects of poverty were more sustained. Especially important in bringing the plight of the poor to the notice of the middle-classes and the political establishment were a series of articles published in the *Morning Post* under the title of 'London Horrors' by John Hollingshead. Unless some steps were taken to improve conditions in the East End, Hollingshead promised, riots would spread and undermine the stability of the nation. Only a few clergymen, doctors and parochial officers, he wrote, knew anything about the depth of poverty in Shoreditch, Bethnal Green, and Spitalfields, of how a 'large mass of trained industry suddenly felt itself displaced' by goods manufactured abroad. Hollingshead relied heavily on the eyewitness accounts of the district's clergy, who guided him through the worst slums.[55]

MINISTERING TO THE NEW POPULATION

In the late twentieth century, churches play a secondary role in welfare provision. In the last century, the situation was reversed. Such provisions as were available came under the control of special parish Vestry boards, Anglican vicars, or Dissenting congregations and their ministers. Churches played a central role in the distribution of social services in overcrowded and poor areas like Hoxton. Only in the late nineteenth century did Parliamentary Acts enable local government to take up the crusade against poverty.

In response to the first signs of population growth in the 1810s and 1820s, Shoreditch Vestry did as many others suburban parishes were doing and built new Anglican chapels using funds made available by the 1818 Church Building Act. The Act allocated £1,000,000 for the construction of new churches in rapidly expanding districts across the Nation.[56] The Commission set up to administer the Act had a dual role, both to review grants applications and to encourage vestries to raise the money locally.

In a letter dated 10 December 1818, the vestry of St Leonard's and the vicar, the Rev. Henry Plumley, asked for grants to meet the total cost of two new churches in Shoreditch. The Commission was loathe to foot the entire bill and wrangled with the Vestry for the next four years.

The Vestry, which maintained that the parish was too poor to contribute much to the project, persuaded the Commission to contribute the major part of the money for St John the Baptist, the design of which went to the architect Francis Edwards in 1823. The site was purchased from H. C. Sturt, the largest landowner in the new district, for 1,000 guineas.[57] St Mary's Haggerston was started at about the same time. It has since been demolished.

The Church of St John the Baptist, New North Road was consecrated on 26 April, 1826 [*figure 21*]. Like most so-called Commissioners' Churches built in cities it had an enormous capacity, with seats for 2,000 worshippers. The total cost including the burial ground opened in 1831 came to £16,444, £13,000 of which came as an outright grant from the Commissioners. The design is compact and logical, admirable for the very lack of superfluous features and ornaments

21 *St John the Baptist's, Hoxton, New North Road. 1823-6, to designs by Francis Edwards. Photo Author.*

which might detract from its gravity. Inexpensive stock brick is used throughout; more costly carved stonework is restricted to points of emphasis in the design. Each part is clearly articulated by giant Tuscan pilasters – porch bays, entrances, chancel and sanctuary. The heavy, broad entablature, like the unrelieved brick, strikes a constant note pulling together disparate elements. The most prominent and obviously church-like feature is the west tower which rises through one square stage, the corners of which rebate and then round off before terminating in a dome.[58]

The creation of a new ecclesiastical district in Hoxton was to be the first of many subdivisions. Throughout the nineteenth century, zealous Anglican clergymen tirelessly campaigned for more ecclesiastical districts and churches in an attempt to keep pace with rapid population growth in the cities. The atomization of the ministry into smaller and smaller units in the most densely populated and most destitute areas of the nation was undertaken in part out of the belief that 'the poor and labouring classes', as the phrase went, stayed away from the Church or shifted their allegiance to Nonconformist churches because of a lack of Anglican provision. If a seat were provided for every inhabitant of church-going age, the population would naturally find their way into the Established Church. Greater Church attendance was believed to improve the conditions of the poor who were thought to be suffering from intemperance and a lack of moderation as much as from the lack of decently paid work or social provision. This neat social equation was a commonplace in the writings of early Victorian Churchmen, but as the century progressed, and particularly after 1850, it became clear that a simple increase in the number of Anglican Churches could not restore the Church to the centre of national life.

In the late twentieth century, it is perhaps hard to imagine how a new parish church could solve social problems. In the nineteenth century, however, when there were few public health officials or hospitals to say nothing of social services or the benefits system, clergy were militant advocates for the poor, publicising their plight among the wealthy and politically influential classes and encouraging the first generation of social workers. The power of this advocacy should not be discounted. The Anglican clergy, and in particular those attracted to slum mission work, tended to be Oxbridge-educated and bred among the ruling classes, perfectly placed, in other words, to sway the opinion of the politically powerful classes. The impact of the Nonconformist clergy was also great but fewer Nonconformist structures survive as witnesses to their activities.

Population growth and the spread of poverty drove Anglicans and Nonconformists relentlessly forward and nowhere was this competition more pronounced than in Hoxton. Many more monuments to Anglican fervour survive, from the Church of St John the Baptist to St Anne's, Holy Trinity, and St Columba's, a reflection of the fact that Anglican churches were usually built with endowments funded by national or diocesan campaigns and then vested with the Bishop or in a trust. By contrast Nonconformist churches tended to be built with the congregation's own money, often augmented by a grant from a national fund. Most of this money went to the building itself so that when a congregation left or grew too poor to support the church, the body of the church wasted away. The only witness to Dissenting activity in the area today is St Monica's Roman Catholic Church and Schools in Hoxton Square, a superb grouping that illustrates the elasticity of the Gothic Revival style when applied to religious, educational and domestic buildings.

The greater survival rate of Anglican structures is misleading, since it was the Nonconformists who responded more quickly to the shifts in population and social changes. The Established Church was encumbered by an elaborate administrative structure, a hierarchy and its status as the official Church which required buildings reflecting its position in society. Nonconformists did not need a Parliamentary Act to put up a meeting house and were not as afflicted by the need to make architectural gestures that expressed a venerable tradition. In 1789, more than thirty years before the construction of St John the Baptist's, the Methodists opened a meeting house in Hoxton Street, the very heart of Hoxton's labouring population [*figure 10*]. This congregation quickly established almshouses funded by donations of the members themselves. How different was St John's, built in a park-like setting with speculative middle-class housing going up on all sides. Indeed the construction of St John's was delayed by four years while funds were sought to provide a church which was stately and grave.

The Methodists in particular would make the New North Road and its adjacent streets a battleground, where Nonconformists and Anglicans struggled to gain the upper hand in the war for souls and against poverty. So keen was the struggle that at times the Nonconformists took up arms against one another. In 1832 the Reeves Place Chapel congregation built a large Sunday School in nearby Ivy Lane. In the same year, a new Methodist congregation arrived in Hoxton and built a simply designed chapel on the east side of the New North Road, near present-day Rushton Street, the Pavement or Barbican

Chapel, named after a chapel which stood in the Pavement, Moorfields.

Hoxton's third Methodist chapel was built in 1839-40 on the east side of New North Road at the corner of Mintern Street, in clear view of St John the Baptist and not one hundred feet from the modest Pavement Chapel. The New North Road Chapel was the most elaborate Dissenting chapel seen so far in the district and was modelled on English churches built in the Romanesque style, the chief characteristic of which is the use of round-arched openings, simply and boldly moulded, with clasping buttresses [*figure 22*]. The entrance was set in a full-height, arched recess, a feature borrowed directly from the west front of an ancient medieval and now Anglican church, Tewkesbury Abbey.

In 1848, the congregation which worshipped in the Pavement Chapel replaced their modest preaching box with what a contemporary observer called a "large, handsome and commodious chapel" in brick. It was built to the designs of B. A. C. Herring in a round-arched style that was based on Italian rather than English Romanesque churches and intended to be the first of three similar church and school complexes projected by the First London Circuit of Methodists [*figure 23*]. For all its pretence and grandeur, however, the public face of the new Pavement Chapel was limited to just one thin strip of an elevation set in line with terraced houses of a common type.[59] Sunday Schools were added in 1874, by which time another large Methodist Chapel was erected in Hoxton, this one adjoining the first Old Street County Court, not far from the Vinegar Works, making a total of four in all.[60]

The Methodists were able to afford some architectural character and willing to erect their chapels on a prominent thoroughfare close by the buildings of the Established Church. To judge from Cox's detailed observations made between 1870 and 1873, the chapels of other Dissenting congregations had little in the way of architectural interest. There was a Baptist meeting hall in Dorchester Place by 1845, but this wealthy congregation left Hoxton for the more suburban climes of Islington in 1853.[61] The Strict Baptists who had built Trinity Chapel, Phillipp Street in 1848 moved to Zion Chapel in Matthias Road, Stoke Newington. Apart from the Methodists, the only Dissenters with a church of definite character was an Independent congregation calling themselves the Bible Christians, who built the Jubilee Chapel in about 1870 at the north end of East Road just around the corner from St John's.[62]

The Nonconformists of Hoxton were extremely successful in their missionary activities. Missions

22 *New North Road Methodist Chapel, 1839-40. Architect unknown.*

were run from small rooms, often ordinary commercial premises. The services were simple, consisting of hymns, a reading perhaps and then a sermon. The informality and immediacy of mission worship was said to be very popular amongst the poor, who, according to contemporary observers, were not comfortable with the elaborate liturgy of the Church of England. The first missions in Hoxton were established in the 1840s, and within a few decades Dissenters from wealthier Islington and Stoke Newington were setting up missions in the East End. In 1870, the Grosvenor Park Presbyterian Church of Islington set up a mission in Hoxton because there were no poor in their own district. In 1884, the Harecourt Congregational Chapel set up a mission for 150 people in Hammond Square Hoxton, near the Ragged School (see below).[63] Because mission work was conducted informally and rarely in specially-built structures, it is difficult to gauge the extent of it. The evidence available suggests that missionary activity

23 *The 'Pavement' Methodist Chapel, New North Road, 1848. Designed by B.A.C. Herring.*

was widespread, especially in the second half of the century. The Anglican and Nonconformist churches, then, were fixed points in the architectural and social topography of Hoxton. Nonconformist missions, which were better able to adapt to changes in the population, were no less important in the life of the community but they were often ephemeral, a fact which explains why so little is known about them. Their success was undeniable, at least to Anglicans, and persuaded many Church of England clergymen to adopt orders of service and techniques closely modelled on those used in Dissenting Missions.[64] Missions were also centres for rudimentary education and other voluntary social services. Some missions eventually became so successful that they commissioned permanent buildings to serve as a base for their activities. Sadly very few of these multipurpose structures survive.

An important Nonconformist Mission in Hoxton was started in 1881 by John and Lewis Burtt. From their premises in the basement of a house, they concentrated on building a close relationship with Hoxton's youth, distributing clothes and food at the same time as friendly guidance. The mission moved to a commercial building on the east side of Hoxton Market in 1886, an area notorious for its pickpockets and children's street gangs. Meetings were held in the Hoxton Market Christian Mission each day and social services dispensed. The Mission was enlarged in 1905 and refronted in 1915 [*figure 24*]. The start of war saw a broadening of social services, including regular soup kitchens, the distribution of boots and holiday meals, classes on health and child care. The Mission encouraged and supported emigration as a solution to deprivation. Children continued to be the focus of work. In 1937 a children's convalescent home was set up in the Sussex countryside.

The interior of the Mission Building was completely destroyed by a bomb in 1941. Luckily the exterior was not harmed. It is a clever design inspired by the once numerous eighteenth-century houses in the nearby squares. Indeed, the windows on the Coronet Street elevation to the rear form a fine closure to the view from Hoxton Square. Returning to the main elevation, the right-hand side and attic reproduce the order and clarity of the early eighteenth-century prototypes; the harmony falls apart on the left, where the openings change scale and axis, forming staggered pairs which light a full-height stair and suggest the image of a polite seventeenth-century house slipping down a steep slope. The paired entrances repeat the doubled rhythm of the stair windows. Unfortunately preliminary research has not revealed the name of the imaginative Edwardian architect. Today the structure has been given over to commercial uses.

The great activity of the Nonconformists in Hoxton, who first began to challenge Anglican authority with several large chapels opened between the 1830s and the 1850s and who followed up chapel building with aggressive mission work during the 1860s, persuaded the Anglicans to take further action, leaving Hoxton with a total of nine Anglican churches, an unusually large number for such a small area. The plainest of this collection was just as grand as the most elaborate Dissenting church in the district; the most distinguished, St Columba's and St Saviour's (sadly demolished in the 1950s), were works of architecture of the first order.

The method of funding these new churches was considerably different from the block-grant system which built St John the Baptist's, New North Road and the other Commissioners' Churches of the 1820s and early 1830s. In the early Victorian period, grants from the Church Building Commission and the Incorporated Church Building Society (founded in 1818) grew smaller. Diocesan church building societies were founded to make grants, but the amounts given tended to be small. Generous grants were available to many

24 *Hoxton Market Christian Mission, Hoxton Market, 1905-1915. Photo Author.*

poor, inner-city parished from special funds set up by local Anglican hierarchy. In general, however, parish authorities were expected to raise the larger part of the construction costs by a local subscription or by a church rate. Since the rate was very unpopular and often the cause of violent protest, it was rarely levied, and when it was it was usually designated 'voluntary'. Church rates were abolished in legislation of 1868, leaving the subscription as the most important source of funds available to vicars seeking to build a new church or enlarge an old one. The clergy of the Church of England became remarkably successful at running national and local campaigns, tapping the great collective wealth of Anglican landowners and businessmen.

The Bishop of London, the Rev. Charles J. Blomfield, appointed in 1828, was a great advocate of church extension schemes in poor parishes funded in part by voluntary contributions and in part from diocesan grant. In 1836, he established the Metropolitan Churches Fund, which made sizeable grants to the construction of 78 new churches over the next twelve years. Blomfield focused his efforts in the East End. His most famous church extension scheme was in Bethnal Green, which received ten new churches by 1848.[65]

The Metropolitan Churches Fund contributed to the erection of Christ Church, Hoxton, facing the New North Road, just north of the Barbican Chapel in what is now Shoreditch Park. The church was completed in 1839 as a Chapel of Ease; two years later it was made the centre of a ecclesiastical district consisting of 8,000 people. Christ Church was Romanesque in style, simply ornamented and made from that most economical of materials, brick. The vicarage was built on the south corner of the site and the National School on the north. There were sittings for more than an thousand worshippers, close to half of which were free to the public. It was customary for places in Anglican churches to be let annually or even sold for personal use, which explains why Anglicans made the provision of free seats one of the goals of slum church building. It was argued that the practice of letting pews kept the poor from worshipping at the parish church.

1848 saw the completion of two more churches aided by the Metropolitan Churches Fund. St Mark's Church was built on the northeast corner of the City Road and Old Street on a site purchased from the Vinegar Works [*figure 25*]. It had a tower projecting from the south aisle of the four-bay nave which ran parallel to the City Road. The design of Benjamin Ferrey, one of the period's leading church architects, was in the early Gothic or First Pointed style, his favourite

25 *St Mark's Old Street, 1848, to the designs of Benjamin Ferrey. One of the Anglican churches aided by Bishop Blomfield's Metropolitan Churches Fund.*

idiom.[66] All of its 1000 seats were free. It was built on speculation, as it were, without a congregation in the hope that a fine new church would attract worshippers. Holy Trinity, Shepherdess Walk, was built under precisely the same circumstances and in almost exactly the same style by William Railton: its tall tower was also calculated to make a strong impact on the streetscape. The materials used in both cases were Kentish Ragstone, more at home in country than city churches.[67]

Church extension aided by the Metropolitan Churches Fund fell off after 1849 as its funds became depleted. The gauntlet was taken up again by a new diocesan, Bishop Tait, who inaugurated a special London fund in 1854, the first year of his episcopacy. He relaunched Blomfield's Fund as the London Diocesan Church Building Society, which attracted promises of £170,000 in its first two years. Tait redoubled his efforts in 1863, promising to raise £500,000 for a newly created 'Bishop of London's Fund for Providing for the Spiritual Wants of the Metropolis'.[68] The creation of a special fund had been suggested by the 1858 House of Lord's *Report on Spiritual Destitution in London*, which singled out the parishes of Clerkenwell, Haggerston, Hoxton, Shoreditch and Stepney as most in need of churches. Bishop Tait wanted one clergyman for every 2,000 inhabitants of the East End and churchroom for one person in every four.[69]

Two of the forty churches aided by Bishop Tait's Fund were in Hoxton: St Andrew's on Canal Road (now Kenning Terrace) completed in 1865 to designs by C.A. Long and St Anne's Hoxton Street consecrated in May of 1870 and designed by Francis Chambers.[70] St Anne's is built from brick but faced in ragstone, giving the appearance of a country church. Like St John's, Christ Church and St Mark's it sought to dominate the streetscape. A polygonal apse rises from low vestries; a high bell tower was planned but never completed for want of funds. The stump of the tower survives as a memorial to the optimism with which Anglicans pursued church building, planning numerous churches with grand features and praying that the money would somehow be found. Too often it was not.

Both Bishop Blomfield and his successor Bishop Tait were opposed to one current in the Anglican practice of their day, an ethos which developed in the 1850s and came to be known as 'Ritualism' because its adherents favoured elaborate ceremonies and tended towards doctrines and practices associated with Roman Catholicism. The success of anti-ritualists such as Blomfield and Tait in building churches which were in their patronage was painful to the Rev. Thomas Simpson Evans, Vicar of Shoreditch and the Rev. John Ross, Vicar of Haggerston both of whom planned a Ritualist mission in Shoreditch. They soon drew Robert Brett and Richard Foster, famed for promoting Ritualism in Stoke Newington, into their scheme. The four established the Haggerston Church Extension Scheme in 1863 to provide the East End with churches practising a 'Prayerbook System of Worship'. To help the scheme on its way Brett gave the royalties earned from his devotional books. Five churches in all were built before 1870: St Chad's, St Columba's, and St Stephen's, all of which came within the parish of Haggerston, St Michael's Shoreditch and St

26 *St Saviour's Hoxton, 1863-70, to the designs of James Brooks.*

Saviour's Hoxton. The architect of these churches was James Brooks, a resident of Stoke Newington. The patronage of the Haggerston Church Scheme churches was vested in a trust for sixty years to ensure that ritualist worship would continue.

The prototype for these churches was St Matthias in Wordsworth Road, Stoke Newington, built in 1851 to designs by William Butterfield and paid for by Dr Brett: broad brick exteriors relieved by judiciously placed stone dressings and ornament; high proportions and striking bold shapes, with aisles reduced to simple lean-to structures and a high clerestory. The skill of the architect consisted in sensing the right sizes and proportions of each part and in arranging the elements of the building almost as one combines shapes to form a pleasing abstract composition. The unique characteristics of town as opposed to city churches was hotly debated in the early 1850s. The work of Butterfield, G. E. Street and William White was instrumental in defining the new sensibility. In St Saviour's [*figure 26*] Brooks took Butterfield's primitivism one step further, paring down exterior mouldings, replacing traceried lights with plate tracery and forging nave and chancel into a single high vessel terminating at the altar in a sweeping round apse. St Saviour's, one of his finest works in this mode, was demolished in 1954. Its parish consisted of streets obliterated to create Shoreditch Park.[71]

Happily, Brooks' masterpiece, perhaps one of the age's greatest town churches, St Columba's (which belongs more properly to Haggerston than Hoxton) does survive. It was consecrated in July of 1869. The complex of clergy house and school around the courtyard to the north was completed by 1873. The great pyramidal roof over the crossing was meant to be first stage of a massive spire which was never built. The techniques used in St Saviour's are here brought to a pitch and intensity rarely matched in High Victorian design: towering masses which seem to bulge out and overwhelm; sheer dense brickwork laid with fine joints; ornament which is tightly bound to the wall surface; a deliberately changeful and asymmetrical elevation; and abrupt shifts in scale, particularly in window openings. In 1872, Charles Eastlake, Secretary of the Royal Institute of British Architects, praised the design in his *History of the Gothic Revival* but noted that its location in a poor and deprived area made it unlikely that many Londoners would visit it.[72] Members of the Architectural Association organised several tours of Brooks' East End Churches. One in August of 1869 was led by the architect himself. The correspondent for the *Building News* who attended the first tour singled out St Columba's for praise

> Placed close to a gigantic workhouse [St Leonard's], Mr. Brooks has outdone his previous works in vigour and simplicity, in order that his building might hold its own and not appear dwarfed by its colossal neighbour.

Climbing its tower, the group could look out at all of Brooks commissions at once. Their 'lofty and fine proportions, with an absence of elaborate detail' made the buildings modern and 'not copies of ancient examples'.[73]

27 *St. Peter's Hoxton Square, 1877, to the designs of Robert Drew. Mission and vicarage established in 1874.*

The last town church built in Hoxton was St Peter's Hoxton Square, completed in 1877 to designs of Robert Drew [*figure 27*]. Sadly, it has gone. The shallow chancel took up the northwest corner of the Square with the long north aisle returned down Bowling Green Walk. At least Drew's vicarage, no.10 Hoxton Square, remains. The use of pointed arches and the elegant triangular first-floor bay rising from a canopied shaft are typical for the date and building type. Of particular note is the top floor, where brick lacing courses are arranged along the lines of timber framing, the wattle and daub panels replaced by dimpled cement. This witty translation of ancient forms into modern industrial materials fits in perfectly with the elegant, spare industrial buildings to the south, nos.8 and 9. The latter is dated 1897, and the former, to judge by its style, is roughly contemporary. The great expanse of windows and bare-bones style are typical of commercial warehouse and light industrial structures from the turn of the century, quite different from nos.5 and 6 which are slightly earlier, from about 1880. This run of buildings demonstrates just how at home brick 'town churches' of the 1870s were in industrial areas.

Fortunately the north side of the square preserves the character of an urban slum mission complex. St Monica's Catholic Church forms the centre of a splendid group [*figure 28*]. Its narrow elevation crowned by a high shouldered bell cote is tightly packed into this crowded site, squeezed between the National Schools to the left and the convent to the right like a commuter standing on a rush-hour train. The design of the School shows just how much architectural interest can be generated by paying attention to proportions, varying the widths of window openings and judiciously placing details. The single thin buttress at the centre of the facade has no structural purpose; it serves only as trunk from which sprouts a black brick cross framed by a narrow gable. The convent is appropriately more self-effacing; the vicarage is located in the southeast corner, at no.36, and serves as a counterpoint to the Anglican residence diagonally opposite.

SCHOOL BUILDING

Just as the Nonconformists were first off the mark in church extension so too did they make the first provisions for education in the district. As was the case with church building, the Anglicans eventually overtook and then overwhelmed the competition, but only very late in the race. The charity school in Aske's Hospital was run as an Anglican Institution and required scholars to attend regular services in the School Chapel. However, the School was not set up to serve the inhabitants of Shoreditch specifically. It received pupils from other parishes and the places were in the gift of the Haberdashers' Company. By contrast the Orphans' Working School was founded for the children of Shoreditch's Protestant Dissenters in 1758 by voluntary subscription. There were 20 places for boys; the same number of girl scholars was soon admitted. By 1775 the school filled three houses and had to move to new, larger premises designed for 100

28 *St Monica's Roman Catholic Church, former National Schools and convent, Hoxton Square, constructed during the 1870s. Photo Author.*

children in the City Road. In 1847 it moved to Haverstock Hill occupying a new building with places for 240 children.[74]

A great improvement in the education of the poor and working classes came not from full-time institutions run by subscription but from Dissenting Sunday Schools which charged very small fees payable each week or monthly. One Sunday School opened in Hoxton Square by 1785, followed by several others in the first half of the next century. The Baptists had run a school for a short time in the 1790s in a house in Hoxton Square, before relocating to Pullins Row, Islington.[75] Although the instruction was religious, the students were taught how to read and write. Good students were encouraged to enter full-time education.[76] Sunday Schools multiplied quickly in Victorian Hoxton. A Wesleyan Sunday School was erected in Ivy Lane in the summer of 1832 and another off the New North Road in 1864. The Presbyterian Grosvenor Avenue Congregation in Highbury built a mission and Sunday School in Hoxton's Albert Square in 1870. The Harvey Street Mission started a Sunday School at about the same time. Once again, the Methodists made a greater impact on the religious topography of the area than any other Protestant sect.[77]

The most influential Nonconformist schools were those started by Thomas Cranfield in Goswell Street. In 1791 he moved to Kingsland Road and opened a Sunday School run by volunteers. He soon had more than 60 pupils, who attended for free. The National Sunday School Union students had to pay fees. By the turn of the century Cranfield had established 19 schools in North London, and then he turned his attention to Southwark where he combined the schools with soup kitchens. In 1844 the volunteer workers who ran these schools formed the Ragged School Union, an interdenominational body to maintain a school inspectorate and make small grants to the establishment of schools. The Union strongly encouraged its members to offer social work services in addition to preaching and basic education. It refused, however, to intervene directly in the internal administration of the school. Lord Anthony Ashley Cooper, later seventh Earl of Shaftesbury and a noted worker for progressive social reforms, was invited to be president.[78] The Hoxton Ragged School entered the Union in 1846 when it was located in a small room on Phillipp Street. The largest landowner in the parish, H.C. Sturt donated a parcel of land in Hammond Square for the construction of a new building which was built with donations from the Ragged School Union, H.C. Sturt and other 'benevolent individuals'.[79] It was completed in 1850 to designs by the architect John Tarring.

The Builder described the brick building with stone dressings as 'plain but spacious . . . in the Tudor style'.[80] There was even an open wood roof and stained glass windows. It was built to serve 400 students.

The Anglicans were eventually more successful as the first providers of inexpensive, full-time education. The National Society for Education in the Principles of the Established Church, or as it was more simply known, the National Society, was founded in 1811 to make grants to the construction and endowment of parish schools where the poor could receive primary education for modest fees. In 1833 the government offered the National Society and the British and Foreign School Society a joint grant of £20,000. The grant was renewed annually and eventually amounted to more than £800,000 in 1861, by which time the National Society was also charged with distributing government funds to other denominations. The Roman Catholics and Methodists built and ran many National Schools.[81]

Public money for education soon brought state intervention. In 1839 the Privy Council on Education, known as the Committee of Council, was formed to organise the distribution of all public money spent on education. The Committee's recommendation of a state school inspectorate was accepted in principle, but political wrangling in the House of Commons exempted Church of England Schools from state inspection. In 1842 the Diocese of London established a Board of Education which ran a school inspectorate. Supporters of secular education and Nonconformist schools pointed out that the Diocesan inspectors would be less critical than those appointed by the state. The victory for Church control was temporary. In 1846 the Committee of Council set up a teacher training system, laying down rules for assistant teachers in 1850. In 1859, the supporters of state inspections won a concession: only schools open to state inspection would qualify for grants to fund building works; government inspection became the rule in 1861.[82]

The first National School in Hoxton was opened in 1822 in an alley off Mundy Street, near Hoxton Square. By the end of the century it served 800 students.[83] (A twentieth-century school occupies the site.) Like later National Schools, the Mundy Street School was supported by voluntary subscriptions, fees paid weekly and later monthly, by special offertory sermons, and by a grant from the National Society. Two more Anglican schools followed: Christ Church National School opened in 1839 and St John the Baptist's National School in 1843.[84] The

29 *National Schools, St John the Baptist, Hoxton, 1842-3, to designs by Lee and Duesbury.*

30 *West wing of Holy Trinity National Schools, Shepherdess Walk, 1864. Photo Author.*

architects of the the latter were Lee and Duesbury, whose design was described by one contemporary reviewer as being in the 'Tudor Domestic' style. [*figure 29*]. It had places for 600 students and the final bill came to £1,849.[85] Tuition was 1 d. per week for Infants and 2 d. per week for all others. Additional children from the same family were charged 1 d. The school also served as a centre for social services, including a Mothers' Group and Penny Savings Bank.

A second bout of Anglican school building started in 1857, when a National School was opened in the yard facing St Mark's. The vicar of St Mark's had been he recipient of an especially large grant made by the Committee of Council to meet new, more stringent school building regulations.[86] Holy Trinity National Schools [*figure 30*], built to the north of the church, opened in 1864, with much of the building work given freely by local craftsmen. The plan is H-shaped and the design rather plain. St Columba's National Schools were finished in 1873, and St Saviour's [figure 31] in 1874, both to designs by James Brooks. The latter was praised in the *Building News* which published a woodcut of the elevation.[87] In June of 1874 Brooks himself led colleagues from the Architectural Association on a tour of East End National Schools.[88]

Brooks' National School for St Saviour's Hoxton was one of the last generation of parish schools. In the early 1870s, local authorities assumed greater control of primary education under the terms of the 1870 Education Act which authorised the creation of local School Boards to build and manage schools. Although the Act did not set out to destroy the voluntary system, voluntary schools were soon competing with the School Board Schools for their very existence. The voluntary system suffered from restricted budgets, made tighter by the abolition of all school fees in

31 *St. Saviour's National Schools, 1873, to the designs of James Brooks.*

1891. Although the London School Board had no stated policy to compete with the voluntary system, it very often built schools near the National Schools in what seemed like a deliberate bid to attract students from them. By 1896, the LSB had built four schools in Hoxton; these were enlarged after 1904 by the London County Council. All of the School Board Schools survive. The Hammond Square Schools, opposite Nuttall Street, the Hoxton House Schools, the Pitfield Street Schools, and the Gopsall Street Schools are all fine designs but have been robbed of their original context by post-war redevelopment. The School Board Schools were designed to tower above the working class neighbourhoods in which they were built, as citadels symbolizing the advance of the secular public welfare system. Something of this shining image of progress can be glimpsed if one stands in Shoreditch Park and looks east towards the façade of Gopsall Street Schools (now the Whitmore School). Its bulk rises high above the forlorn terrace of houses in Bridport Place.

Some National Schools closed almost as soon as the local Board School opened. Others decided that it was better to make themselves over to the local Board than to close entirely. By 1905 only five of the once numerous the National Schools in Hoxton – Christ Church, St Saviour's, St John's, St Columba's and St Monica's – were open. In that year St Saviour's was absorbed by the London County Council, which succeeded the LSB as the metropolis' chief education provider in 1904. St John's Schools gradually lost its autonomy in order to take advantage of the LCC building grants; the 1840s complex was overhauled in 1908 and served until 1966. The National Schools also lost teachers to the Board Schools which paid better salaries.[89] The buildings which housed the Holy Trinity, St Peter's, St Monica's and St Columba's schools survive.

PUBLIC FACILITIES AND UTILITIES

The last decade of the nineteenth century witnessed the emergence of facilities – free state schools, parks, libraries, baths, and housing – run for the public good from a mixture of grants,

[33]

user fees and local rates. Parish vestries –which assumed the form of what we would recognize as local government over the course of the century – gradually took the lead in establishing such services. The Shoreditch Vestry's powers were increased by the Shoreditch Improvements Act of 1872, but conditions were slow to change.[90] A pure water supply, for example, was only secured in the 1880s. Advances were hastened by a steady increase in the rateable value of Shoreditch.[91]

By 1860 all the open land in Hoxton had been built over leaving no space for recreation apart from the private squares at the south end. The area's first public park was the churchyard of St John the Baptist's which was opened for public use in 1882. In 1893 Goldsmith's Recreation ground was opened under the auspices of the Metropolitan Public Gardens Association who, in 1900, also paid for the removal of gravestones from St John the Baptist's churchyard freeing it for recreation.[92] In 1898 the Housing Commission of Shoreditch Vestry opened Charles Square for public use. The LCC contributed to the purchase of the site from the landowner. By 1916, Hoxton Square, Aske Gardens, and Geffrye Gardens in Haggerston had been added to the list of open spaces.[93] Still, the amount of open space was inadequate until the start of the construction of Shoreditch Park in the 1960s.

The grandest Shoreditch Vestry scheme was the construction of a single complex uniting a public library, baths and a refuse disposal system. The refuse was to be burned to provide steam to heat the baths and library and to drive turbines to generate electricity. This bold undertaking was the result of several earlier attempts to build public baths in Hoxton. As early as 1852 the vestry had adopted the terms of the 1846 Public Baths and Washhouses Act. A Commission was appointed in 1854 and three sites along major thoroughfares were considered. The most suitable was owned by the Ecclesiastical Commissioners but their asking price was too great. Plans were laid aside until 1876 when the chairman of a new Committee hit upon a site at the south end of Pitfield Street.

It took eleven years for the vestry to approve a more detailed study, which was published in 1887. The Pitfield Street site could be had for £10,000 and a building provided for £20,000 or £30,000. The money could be borrowed from the Local Government Board and day-to-day costs paid out of local rates. Both the principal and the operating costs were to be recovered from admission charges. All washhouses built in London since the one in Greenwich which opened in 1852 were financed in this way, but not all could meet their obligations. The Shoreditch Vestry and Washhouse Committee wanted to make sure that their facility would not be a strain on the ratepayers.[94] Despite the assurances offered in the 1887 report, another eight years would pass before the start of construction.

In 1895 the vestry ran an architectural competition for the design of the Baths and Washhouses; the assessor was Rowland Plumbe, FRIBA. The first prize and the commission went to Henry Thomas Hare (1861-1921) who came to specialise in the design of every manner of public building from Carnegie Libraries to police and fire stations. Despite Hare's talent, he was not, as the Committee was quick to point, a specialist in planning baths. The firm of Spalding and Cross, whose design had not even been selected for honourable mention, were pioneers in the planning of such buildings and their plan for the Pitfield Street Baths had, in the opinion of the Bath House Committee, greater merit than any other. The commission for the exterior was awarded to Hare and for the plan to Spalding and Cross with the baths opening in 1899 [*figure 32*]. The London-based partnership of Spalding and Cross was formed in 1889. Alfred Cross went on to become a leading expert on the design of public baths, publishing the standard work on the subject, *Public Baths and Wash-houses*, in 1906. The only surviving baths by the firm in London are those in Whiston Road, Haggerston, of 1903-4.

It is astonishing to think that more than forty years passed between the vestry's adoption of the 1846 Act and the selection of an appropriate site. Since the 1850s, the parish Health Officer had been calling for an improvement in sanitary facilities. The tenements thrown up in the 1850s and 1860s had very poor drainage and some no drainage at all. Where did the poor in Hoxton go to bathe? Since the seventeenth century, there had been a natural spring on the south side of Old Street, opposite the bottom of Pitfield Street. In 1745 Chassereau noted that the spring was feeding a 'cold bath and much frequented for the care of rheumatic pains'. The baths were larger than any in eighteenth-century London, some 20 x 30 feet, and were expanded in the next century. Cox described them in his 1873 survey, though it appears some of the water was then being diverted for a local industry. In any case, the unheated facilities were not large enough to serve the district's inhabitants.[95]

Sometime in the early 1890s, the Washhouse project was linked with plans to construct a refuse burning and electric generating plant on the north side of Hoxton Market. It is not clear who hit upon the idea to heat and light the Washhouse with steam and electricity generated by burning

:Elevation to Pitfield Street:

rubbish. The elegance and economy of the scheme is appealing even today. The construction of a refuse destructor had been projected in 1891 and proceeded, in contrast to the Washhouse project, with all possible speed. The Vestry was worried that a private electric generating company would set up a facility and rob the parish of precious revenue. The Board of Trade gave provisional approval to the vestry-run refuse destructor in July 1892. In 1893 the consulting engineer for the project, E. Manville, recommended combining refuse destruction with electrical generating. Attempts to produce steam from refuse burning in order to drive electric turbines were common in the 1890s. The ratepayers endorsed the proposals in 1894 and the site was selected in 1895, the same year as the Pitfield Street Washhouse site. The Hoxton refuse burning station was widely discussed because it was the first specially built to generate steam. Earlier facilities had been converted to steam generating from refuse burning. The plant was opened in June of 1897 by Lord Kelvin. The handsome red brick and terracotta facade to Coronet St contained offices; behind were the destructor hall, storage bins, three Engines and 80 foot stack. The Latin inscription over the

32 & 33 *Henry Hare's designs for the Pitfield Street Baths and Free Library (Passmore Edwards). Published in* The Builder, *December, 1895. (right) Pitfield Street entrance. Demolished 1962-63.*

34 *The Hoxton Market entrance to the Shoreditch Vestry Refuse Destructor and Steam Generating Station, 1895-97, project engineer, E. Manville. Photo Author.*

entrance, *E Pulvere lux et vis*, can be translated as 'Light and Power from Dust' [*figure 33*].[96]

The final component of the municipal site along Pitfield and Coronet Streets was the Pitfield Street Library, a rate for which was approved in March of 1891. Like the Washhouses, it eventually came to be heated and lit by power generated in the nearby refuse destructor plant. Passmore Edwards, who made grants for the construction of public libraries across the country, helped to fund the Pitfield Street Library and the extension of Haggerston Public Library. The foundation stones were laid on the morning and afternoon of same day, 11 June, 1893. Rowland Plumbe was asked to assess an open competition. It seems likely, however, that the competition did not progress very far, because the team responsible for the washhouses, Hare with Spalding and Cross, was selected almost at once. The Library opened in 1896 [*cover*]. It is a masterpiece of turn-of-the-century design, powerfully asymmetrical with an entrance near the corner set in a stout turreted tower. The Dutch gabled bays to the south complemented the facade of the washhouse. The range of materials – brick laid with thin mortar joints, stone banding, and terracotta – are typical for the day. The beauty of the structure derives as much from its lively and varied details and subtle colouring as it does from relative size of its parts and their relation to the larger mass of the building. It is to be regretted that decorative programmes illustrating the work of Shakespeare were never carried out due to a lack of funds. Even sadder to consider is the demolition of the Washouses, which spoiled a truly splendid group. The Washouses had suffered some war damage and reopened in 1951. The old Metropolitan Borough of Shoreditch, however, wanted new facilities and leased the Washouse site to

National Car Parks in 1962 on condition that NCP demolish the structure and take steps to secure the adjacent properties from damage. The party wall with the Library caused particular problems with the result that the work of demolition took more than a year.

The first publicly assisted housing scheme in the parish dates to the early 1890s. Up until this time, the only assisted working-class housing was built by trusts and housing associations formed in the middle of the century. In 1856 Dr Barnes, the Shoreditch Health Officer, lamented that the Society for the Improvement of the Condition of the Working Classes had not yet built any model dwellings in the parish.[97] The Improved Industrial Dwellings Company purchased a site in Tabernacle Square for the construction of houses in 1868, one of the first such schemes in Shoreditch and one of the IIDC's earliest projects.[98] These early efforts were profit-making ventures, financed by low interest loans repaid from rents.

St Leonard's vestry was eager to go into the business of assisted housing by taking advantage of the powers granted parishes and metropolitan boroughs by the Housing of the Working Classes Act of 1890. Under the terms of the Act, the Shoreditch Vestry erected Model Artisans' Dwellings in Moira Place and Plumbers Place, reputed to be the first built by any vestry or District Board of a Metropolitan Borough. In 1897 the Vestry built a village of Cottage Homes in Hornchurch, Essex, as a remedial measure while plans for much-needed large-scale schemes were delayed by disputes over funds promised by the London County Council, which wanted to wrest control of the scheme from the Vestry. A government minister intervened and the two bodies agreed to contribute £27,500 each. At the same time, the Vestry contemplated changing the road pattern in the southwest corner of Hoxton, widening East Road and Provost Street and removing the filthy, ill-lit cul-de-sacs and alleyways lined with tenements.[99] Starting in 1898, 500 residents in four streets of back to back tenements were rehoused; the tenements were destroyed and the Nile Street Market, the second largest in Hoxton, was closed. The Nile Street housing provided two- and three-room dwellings for 400 tenants, a shopping parade and an open space. The architect was Rowland Plumbe, the assessor of the Library and Washhouse competitions. The lavatories were public to allow health officers to monitor their condition in regular inspections, a practical idea but certainly demeaning for the tenants. Rents were also thought to be too high. Construction was complete by 1900. 'The Nile', as it was known, was small by comparison with the first LCC housing estates, in particular the Boundary Estate in Nichol Street, Shoreditch, and it was criticised for this reason.[100] Had the Nile survived, this perceived liability might have become an asset.

Very little council housing was built in Hoxton over the next twenty years despite the fact that the area was ripe for slum clearance. The sale of the Allingham Estate, formerly the Sturt estate and the largest in Hoxton, in 1916 presented the LCC with several opportunities, but its intervention was minimal: forty flats in New North Road, fourteen cottages in Shap Street, and two small blocks in Teale Street were built between 1920 and 1925. The only project whose size was commensurate with the housing problem was the Whitmore Estate, an 8½ acre site built around Ware Street. Conditions in these streets had been worsened by the relocation of tenants here from the Boundary Estate site in Haggerston Road. The LCC started construction in 1924. By 1937 16 blocks with 538 units and 6 shops had been built for £265,000. Many of the original streets were retained and widened. The brick blocks were designed in a Georgian Revival style which is typical of much LCC work between the wars.[101] The numerous post-war estates in Shoreditch, though good examples of their type, are by no means as sensitively scaled as the Whitmore blocks. And it is to be lamented that more recent works throughout London have shown so little regard for the older street patterns.

PENNY GAFFS AND HOXTON'S THEATRES

Through the four centuries of history treated in this essay, one theme has been made clear: Hoxton's proximity to the City has been both a blessing and a curse. It has to be said that since the early nineteenth century this proximity has produced more misery than joy, with the area becoming infamous not only for its poverty but as a centre for East End criminal activity. There were several bright spots in the district, however; by 1850 Hoxton was renowned as a theatre and entertainment district catering to all classes of society.[102] For a time East End theatres came to rival those in the West End. Burbage's first playhouses and the nearby Pimlico Gardens set the stage, as it were, for later developments. The recreation grounds of Islington and Hackney were more salubrious than those in the Hoxton and Shoreditch, which were known for their tavern pleasure gardens where one could stroll, eat, drink, play games, listen to music, or marvel at the skills of street entertainers.

The opening of the City Road in 1761 encouraged the growth of the Shepherd and Shepherdess Tea Gardens at the bottom of Shepherdess Walk. By the turn of the eighteenth century, the Tea Gardens had become the Eagle Tavern, commemorated in the popular nursery rhyme,

> Up and down the City Road,
> In and out the Eagle,
> That's the way the money goes
> Pop! goes the weasel.

During the Regency period, the Eagle ran one of the best known pleasure grounds in London. In 1825, the Grecian Theatre was built within its precincts and later decorated with the stages used for William IV's coronation in Westminster Abbey.

Legally, the Grecian was not yet a theatre. It was licensed as a tavern which allowed light entertainment along with drinking and smoking but limited the size of the venue. In 1843 the Grecian received a saloon licence, which allowed it to build a separate hall with a proper stage. Smoking and drinking were not permitted, as in a theatre, but access to the performance space remained through the tavern. The Grecian received a full theatre licence in the following decade and expanded on a grand scale. When Cox toured Shoreditch in 1873 it was still a spectacular sight and he found it a 'stupendous edifice', recording that it had cost more than £7,000 to build.

The Britannia Theatre had also started as a tea garden which became a tavern and then a saloon before maturing into a theatre.[103] It was founded in the early nineteenth century at the east end of Pimlico Walk in Hoxton Street, an area which was well known for its alehouses. In 1839 Samuel Lane, a Devonshire man who had moved to London in the 1830s and with his wife ran the Union Tavern in Shoreditch, assumed control of the Britannia. There followed four years of frustration as Lane tried to bring serious theatre to Hoxton. In 1841 he erected a stage in the tavern, spending some £3,000 pounds on the conversion, but his application for a music and dancing licence was refused. He reopened the Britannia as a saloon under the terms of the 1843 Theatre Regulations Act and his application for a licence contained a petition of support signed by local inhabitants. This time Lane was successful. His licence was renewed for the next fifteen years, during which time the Britannia developed a strong repertory with stock actors and a good reputation for plays, pantomime and farce. During the late 1840s it attracted respectable audiences from all over London, and in 1850 Charles Dickens began to frequent it. Dickens was impressed by the ease with which all classes of society mixed at the Britannia. In 1856, the indefatigable Lane decided it was time to expand.

35 *Interior of the Britannia Theatre, Hoxton Street and Britannia Gardens, 1856-8, to the designs of Finch, Hill and Paraire*

Before he had even received his theatre licence, he rebuilt the Britannia on a lavish scale to designs by Finch, Hill and Paraire, who provided decor, stage machinery, gas lighting and ventilation to exceptionally high standards. The plan was novel; the hall was elliptical not semicircular or horseshoe shaped. As a result the view from every seat was excellent, or so *The Builder* reported [*figure 34*]. The final cost came to nearly £20,000. A theatre licence was granted in the autumn of 1858, and for the next forty years, the Britannia was one of London's preeminent theatres.

By 1867, the Britannia's success was so great that it emboldened an entrepreneur, Verrall Nunn, to build a competing theatre in Pitfield Street. The Varieties Theatre is the only one of Hoxton's theatre's to survive, though it is has not been in full-time use since 1967. Nunn's scheme failed quickly, and the Varieties was bought by George Harwood (owner of 'The Panorama' in Shoreditch High Street). He changed the Varieties' programme from theatrical performances to a form of entertainment which was native to the East End, Penny Gaff. Gaffs were inexpensive, variety events, comprising comedy, short sketches and songs. The first Gaffs were performed in the early part of the century, in makeshift halls off back alleys or in warehouses.

They attracted the working poor in droves and were considered by reformers to be the cause of serious social problems. The Varieties was also used as a trial house for premiering unknown plays. By the turn of the century it had developed something of a speciality in socialist realist drama.

The third sort of entertainment which thrived in the East End were Music Halls, spaces for variety entertainment where eating and drinking were allowed. The Music Halls of the early nineteenth century were no more than alcoves in public houses. Before very long Music Halls expanded and proved a serious threat to legitimate theatres. The competition between halls and theatres grew so fierce during the early 1840s that established theatres made formal objections to the licensing authorities, claiming that the halls had in effect become theatres which sold alcohol. Threatened with closure for violating licensing agreements, the Music Halls dropped theatrical performances altogether and returned to songs and short comedies. By specialising in this format Music Halls were very popular. Changes in building and safety regulations at the end of the century forced many to close.

Hoxton Street is home to a rare survival of this important East End type, Hoxton Hall, which appears in the Shoreditch Rate Books of 1863 [*figure 35*]. By 1866 the surname of one of the joint proprietors, MacDonald, was applied to the venue, and under his control it had a short and fitful life, being enlarged in 1865, closed in 1872, and then reopened in 1878, only to close for the last time in 1882. The current structure with its U-shaped tiers of galleries carried on cast-iron columns can be dated on stylistic grounds to the 1865 enlargement. The street elevation is barely differentiated from the domestic architecture of the period; it is rather plain, with the exception of a trio of arched openings on the ground floor. In 1885, MacDonald's was purchased by William Goulding, the chairman of a temperance organization called the Blue Ribbon Army. In 1894 Goulding sold it to the Quakers who ran Hoxton Hall as a neighbourhood centre. It is still leased for this purpose, but has been revived in recent years as a venue for theatrical and musical performances.

36 *Hoxton Hall, Hoxton Street, 1863-6.*

Final thoughts on architectural conservation in Hoxton

There is depressingly little left in Hoxton to bear witness to its remarkable and long history. The meandering line of Hoxton Street itself, the irregular alignment of building plots, and the jogging front walls of the buildings themselves allow one to trace something of its changing fortunes and character over five centuries. The small garden recently established along its east side is a reminder of the area's once famous gardens as well as its role as a provider of recreation and fresh produce to City inhabitants. St Anne's, the old workhouse and infirmary, the Hoxton House and Hammond Square Board Schools are all conspicuous monuments, but they have been robbed of their original context by late twentieth-century schemes. The future of the workhouse and hospital sites is, as noted above, uncertain. Their demolition would weaken the character of the area further.

An even graver problem is Hoxton Square. Few areas in London illustrate so startling a transformation of the urban environment over three centuries as does Hoxton with what little is left of its architectural history. St Peter's vicarage by Drew of 1874 as well as nos.32, 49, 50, and 56 Hoxton Square are listed Grade II and rightly so. The St Monica's complex and its vicarage, no.36, are not listed. The case for adding the church, school and convent is a strong one. Every passing year makes them increasingly rarer types. An argument can also be made for listing the surviving industrial buildings along the west side for their group value with the Drew vicarage. The vicarage is valuable precisely because it is at home in an industrial landscape; without the context it becomes meaningless. What should be preserved in Hoxton Square and the surrounding streets are not individual buildings but a collection of types.

There are several other potentially 'listable' structures to the west. The Refuse Destructor and Power Generating Station in Coronet Street is not only historically important but is also a handsome example of its kind, and singlehandedly holds up one side of Hoxton Market. The case for listing has been weakened by the destruction of the baths, which formed a single complex including the Pitfield Street Library, listed Grade II. The Hoxton Market Christian Mission is listable on historic and architectural grounds, although further research is needed to establish the identity of the architect and come up with comparable examples from the same time. The elevation is a remarkably clever design, a reference to Hoxton's early eighteenth-century character. It also stands as a memorial to of the beginnings of the social work movement in the East End of London, in the very place which Charles Booth, more than one hundred years ago, classified as one of the most vice-ridden and deprived areas of in the metropolis.

Experience has shown that the Conservation Area status conferred on Hoxton Street and Hoxton Square does not accord sufficient protection to fragile historic environments. There is now, finally, talk of strengthening Conservation Area legislation. In the meantime, adding structures to the list would increase the area's chances for survival.

To illustrate the importance of listing, one need only walk over to Charles Square and consider its sad fate. No.16, the old County Court, was listed in 1950, one of the first buildings in Hackney designated under the terms of the 1947 Town and Country Planning Act. No other buildings in the Square were designated, nor was any protection afforded them by controls similar to those put into effect by the Conservation Areas Act of 1977. Nothing stood in the way of redevelopment schemes. The neighbours of no.16, some filled with fine panelling documented by the LCC's photographic survey team, fell one after another. The remaining lone red brick facade appears almost comical, wedged into an expanse of concrete framing. The vitality which would have been provided by similar elevations is gone, and the park appears to be a space left over after planning. No. 47 is another likely candidate for addition to the list. It has important townscape value, securing the corner entry to Charles Square, and is an interesting example of an artisan's dwelling erected at the entrance to a polite square. Recommendations for additions to the List are needed, not just for Hoxton but for all of Hackney which is grossly underlisted. While listing does not literally keep historic buldings standing, it does at least bring them within the net of planning controls and is a first step to the conservation of any historic environment.

Endnotes

1 See Hackney Archives Department (hereafter HAD) Map SH 1829.
2 For notes on Hoxton in the Tudor period, see A.S. Travis, 1960, 3-23; W. Wilford, 1966, 5-9; and Cox 1873. Ellis, 1798, contains the most detailed notes on the area's early inhabitants. Volume VIII of the *Survey of London, Shoreditch,* is an invaluable sourcebook.
3 Notes on HAD Maps SH 1764.
4 Travis, 23.
5 *Theatres in Hackney,* exhibition at the Hackney Museum, Winter, 1992-93; R. Sinclair, 146.
6 M. Pelling, 88-90
7 Cox, 271-3.
8 Summerson, *Architecture in Britain,* 164-5.
9 *Tis a Mad World at Hogsdon,* 45.
10 Cox, 231-2.
11 Mitchell and Leys, 172-7.
12 Summerson, *Georgian London,* for the standard account, 27-51.
13 Robinson, 8-9; *Survey of London,* VIII, *Shoreditch,* 137.
14 *Survey,* VIII, *Shoreditch,* 75-6.
15 1929 edition, 19.
16 A. D. Morris, 1957.
17 J.W. Ashley, 122 ff, 172, 186. Cappel was one of many thousands of French Protestants seeking refuge in England after Louis XIV revoked the promise of relgious toleration in 1685. Many French Protestants, called Huguenots, believed that they would be persecuted by the Catholic Church if they remained in France. England seemed a safe haven because the restrictions imposed on Nonconformists were being lifted in these very years. Many of the French immigrants were silk weavers and skilled decorative artists, having been trained in the Royal workshops of France in the arts connected with furniture making. The largest concentration settled in Spitalfields, which became renowned for its fine silks. Hoxton was home to a fair number of Huguenot furniture makers. A French Protestant Church was built in Hoxton Square by 1714. It was maintained by a grant from the Royal Bounty Fund until 1785. On the French Protestant Churches, see Beeman, 3-5, 43-4.
18 V.E. Lipman in Newman, 17, 20.
19 Summerson, *Architecture in Britain,* 178-9.
20 Cox, 1873, 464 and Ware, 1836, 2-4.
21 Illus. in Robinson, 53.
22 Ware, 50-6.
23 Ware, 29-30.
24 Cox, 466; *Survey,* 87; Robinson, 52.
25 Cox, 293, 320, 465; *Survey,* 51.
26 *Victoria County Histories,* 296-8; Cox, 301-7; *Survey,* 141-2.
27 In the course of recent excavations evidence for two earlier houses with brick foundations were unearthed. An original stair is in the course of repair. Later work will concentrate on reinstating the panelled interiors based on paint analysis. Letter from Julian Harrap to the author, May 1993.
28 No.47 was another exceptionally fine specimen. It survives only in the pages of the *Survey of London.*
29 *Survey,* 85, built for James Pitman; Travis, 30 and ff for overview.
30 *London Past and Present,* 246.
31 *Tis a Mad World at Hogsdon,* 45.
32 Cox, 273.
33 Ware, 37-8; Cox, 228.
34 Watercolour of the St Leonard's Workhouse to be found in Vol. II, opposite page 117, in the 'Grangerised Ellis' held in the HAD.
35 *Survey,* 66-7; Cox, 224, 271-3.
36 The City Lying-In Hospital, founded in the late eighteenth century at the corner of Old Street and City Road, was a purely charitable institution. It was adjacent to St Luke's Parish Workhouse.
37 *Report of the Capabilities of the Metropolitan Workhouses for the Reception and Treatment of Cholera,* 35; see E. McKellar for an account of some of these early developments.
38 *The Builder,* 7 June, 1856, 305, 546; *Building News,* 19 March, 1858, 287.
39 *The Builder,* 5 February, 1859, 97.
40 For a complete account see Brassett.
41 *The Builder,* 1863, 694.
42 Further advances in the care of the sick and poor came in 1867 with the Metropolitan Poor Act, which established the Metropolitan Assylums Board. The Board promoted the construction of better equipped and larger workhouse infirmaries controlled by special management boards which were separate from those that ran workhouses. This legislation was instrumental in improving workhouse conditions in the East End. The leading medical journal of the day, *The Lancet,* had been advocating the expansion of workhouse infirmaries into free public hospitals since the early 1860s. See Brewer, 'Workhouse Life in Town and Country', 1872?, pamphlet in HAD, and *The Building News,* 7 July, 1865.
43 The effects of the collapse of the silk weaving industry were still being felt in the 1860s, and were cited by Hollingshead in his famous series of articles, later published under the title, *Ragged London,* 1861, 75-6.
44 The best account of the early nineteenth-century history of Hoxton can be found in the introductory sections of Travis.

45 *Survey*, 76-80.
46 Wilford, 18-20. The toll at the north end was in place until 1863 and at the south until 1868.
47 HAD Map SH 1829 and SH 1839.
48 *Buildings at Risk in Hackney*, 1987, 10-11. Nos. 27 and 29 New North Road were rebuilt in 1903 as the Borough of Shoreditch Constitutional Club to designs by Sydney Cranfield. *The Builder*, 20 February, 1904.
49 See Linda Clarke's important recent study, *Building Capitalism. Historical Change and the Labour Process in the Production of the Built Environment*, 1992.
50 See Hackney Society Publication, *South Shoreditch*, 54-6.
51 Excellent account of these decades found in J. M. Harwood.
52 See Barnes report noted in *The Builder*, 7 July, 1856, 305, 546 and Travis, 1960. James Grant's *Sketches of London*, 1838, noted that the increasing number of poor in the East End of London was a recent phenomenon; as noted in M. Rose, 225-8.
53 HAD Map SH 912:1839.
54 Tyack, 43-66.
55 The letters were published in a single volume titled *Ragged London* in 1861.
56 See 58 George III Cap 45. B.F.L. Clarke introduction and M.H. Port, *Six Hundred New Churches*, 1966.
57 Wilford, 5-22.
58 Reviewed in the *Gentleman's Magazine* for March, 1827. See B.F.L. Clarke, 150 for a list of changes to the fabric.
59 Cox, 326.
60 Cox, 344.
61 By 1872, the Baptists had constructed another chapel at the south end of East Road, at the rear of an alley.
62 *Survey*, 105, and P. Temple, 123 and 129.
63 *Survey*, 105.
64 *Church Builder*, 1864, 66; 1869, 24; 1876, 190-6; 1877, 15-18.
65 B F.L. Clarke, 148-55; *Church Builder*, 1865, 57-61.
66 Mr. Holland of Wanstead was the builder. Cox, 342; undated clipping in the HAD P 3188 212 Mark.
67 Cox, 328, and B.F.L. Clarke, 150.
68 'Ten Years of Church Extension in the Diocese of London', *Church Builder*, 1865, 57-61.
69 'The Bishop of London's Fund', *Church Builder*, 1865, 57-61.
70 *The Church Builder* (1865, 180) reported that St Andrew's had seats for 890 and cost £3,200. It was demolished and the parish amalgamated with St Anne's in 1953. Long designed the new Shoreditch vestry in 1865. It was extended in 1902 as Shoreditch Town Hall.
71 See Harwood.
72 See G. Stamp and C. Amery, *Victorian Buildings of London, 1837-1887. An Illustrated Guide*, London, 1982, 106-8.
73 *Building News*, 30 August, 1869, 379; see also 19 January, 1873, 620, and 26 June, 1874, 711.
74 Cox, 286.
75 *Survey*, 132.
76 Baldry, 35 and ff. The Dissenting Sunday School movement rapidly expanded after the establishment of the Gloucester Dissenting Sunday School in 1780. In 1785, hundreds of schools formed themselves into national Sunday School Union of Dissenters. For a detailed discussion see Thomas Laquer's superb study.
77 The Wesleyan Chapel Committee was founded in 1868 to fund new churches, ministers' houses, and schools. See *Builder*, 1870, 144-6 and *The Fifteenth Report of the Wesleyan Chapel Committee*.
78 Franklin and Bailey, 7-11.
79 Cox, 251-2.
80 1849, 598.
81 Felt, 9-11.
82 Baldry, 46 and ff.
83 Cox, 273.
84 Cox, 308.
85 Cox, 308-11; Wilford, 36 and ff.
86 *Building News*, 9 October, 1857.
87 9 April, 1878, 398.
88 *Building News*, 26 June, 1874, 711.
89 Wilford, 60 and ff.
90 *The Builder*, 1874, 793; *Building News*, 1874, 614.
91 In 1882 railways generated £50,000, the gas works in Whiston Road and Prichard Road £28,000, the Board Schools £5400, and the theatres £1000. *The Builder*, 1882, 415.
92 Wilford, 1966.
93 Travis, 109.
94 *Baths and Washhouses*, Report of the Special Committee to the Vestry of St Leonard's Shoreditch, rev. 1892 ed., HAD L/S/7. See also "Souvenir Programme. The Opening of Public Baths and Washhouses", 18 March 1899, HAD L/V/118 ii.
95 Cox, 344-5; *Survey*, 25-9; and Defoe, 19.
96 Greater London Industrial Archaeology Society, 1986; see also HAD L/V/118 v and *South Shoreditch*, Hackney Society, 54-5.
97 *Builder*, 1856, 305.
98 *Building News*, 1868, 668.
99 In 1893 Arthur Cawston had made sweeping proposals for new roads in the East End, which included a broad road thoroughfare linking the City Road with Columbia Market. See Travis, 69-79.
100 Travis, 61-5.
101 Travis, 61-5.
102 The following account relies heavily on the notes compiled for the exhibition on theatres in Hackney, Hackney Musuem, winter 1992-3; no exhibition catalogue was published.
103 Davis, 1-9.

List of sources cited and consulted

Ashley, J.W., *The Contribution of Dissenting Academies*, London, 1954.
Baldry, J., *The Hackney Free and Parochial Schools*, 1970.
Baths and Washhouses, Report of the Special Committee to the Vestry of St. Leonard's Shoreditch, 1887, revised in 1892.
Beeman, G.B., 'Notes on the Sites and History of the French Churches in London', *Proc. of the Huguenot Society of London*, VIII, 1905, 13-59.
Brassett, D.A., *Saint Leonard's Hospital, 1863-1963*, 1963.
Bryant, M.E., *The London Experience of Secondary Education*, London, 1986.
The Builder, 1841-86.
The Building News, 1853-1886.
The Church Builder, the Journal of the Incorporated Church Building Society, 1861-1881.
Clarke, B.F.L., *Parish Churches of London*, London, 1966.
Cox, J., *An Account of the Parish of St. Leonard's Shoreditch, Middlesex and of the Several Charities and Benefactions to the same...*, manuscript dated August, 1873. HAD M698.
Davis, J., ed., *The Britannia Diaries, 1863-1875*, Society for Theatre Research, 1992.
Defoe, D., *A Tour through London about the Year 1725*, 1929 edition by M.M. Beeton and E. B. Chancellor.
The Ecclesiologist, 1841-1861.
Ellis, Henry, *The History and Antiquities of the Parish of St. Leonard's in Shoreditch and of the Liberty of Norton Folgate*, London, 1798. See also the 'Grangerised' Ellis in HAD.
Felt, A. M., *The London School Board and Elementary Education, with Special Reference to Hackney*, London, 1975.
Franklin, G and D. Bailey, *The History of the Shaftesbury Society, Founded as the Ragged School Union in 1844*, London, the Shaftesbury Society, 1979. Supplement 1989.
Greater London Industrial Archaeological Society, 'Newsletter', 106, supp. October 1986, HAD TQ 331.27.
Hackney Museum, 'Theatres in Hackney', exhibition notes, Winter of 1992-92.
Hackney Society, *Buildings at Risk in Hackney*, 1987.
Hackney Society, *South Shoreditch, Historic and Industrial Buildings*, 1986.
Harwood, J., 'Vanished Church, Vanished Streets: the Parish of St. Saviour's, Hoxton', *East London Historical Society*, no. 9, 1986, 1-19.
Hollingshead, J., *Ragged London*, London, 1861.
Hoxton Market Christian Mission, Hoxton, 1952.
Jay, the Rev.A.O., *A History of Shoreditch*, London, 1896.
Knott, B., *The Hub of Hoxton, 1851-1871*, Hoxton, 1987.
Laquer, T., *Religion and Respectability. Sunday Schools and Working Class Culture*, New Haven, 1978.
London Past and Present, London, 1904.
McKellar, E., *The German Hospital Hackney. A Social and Architectural History*, Hackney Society Publication, 1991.
Mitchell, R.J., and M.D.R. Leys, *A History of London Life*, 1963 edition.
Morris, A.D., *Dissenting Ministers in Hoxton Square*, privately printed, 1957.
Newman, A. ed., *The Jewish East End, 1840-1939*, Jewish Historical Society of England, 1980.
Pelling. M., *The Making of the Metropolis. London 1500-1700*, London, 1986, 88 and ff.
Robinson, E., *Lost Hackney*, Hackney Society Publication, 1989.
Rose, M., *The East End of London*, London, 1951.
Sinclair, R., *East London*, no date.
Stow, J., *A Survey of London*, London, 1603; 1908 edition.
Summerson, J., *Architecture in Britain, 1530-1830*, The Pelican History of Art, 1977 edition.
Summerson, J., *Georgian London*, London, 1978 edition, 1991 printing.
Survey of London, VIII, *Shoreditch*, London, 1922.
Temple, P., *Islington Chapels*, RCHME, London, 1992.
Tis a Mad World at Hogsdon. A Short History of Hoxton, Hoxton Hall, no date.
Travis, A.S., 'Physical Planning and the Borough of Shoreditch, 1880 to the Present', TS in HAD, 1966.
Tyack, J., *Sir James Pennethorne and the Making of Victorian London*, Cambridge, 1992.
Victoria County Histories, Middlesex, I, 1969.
Ware, J., *An Account of the Several Charities and Estates Held in Trust for the Use of the Poor of the Parish of St. Leonard's Shoreditch...*, London, 1836.
Wilford, W., "The History of St. John the Baptist's Church and Schools, Hoxton, 1815-1918", TS in HAD, 1966.
Wilkinson, A., *Antiquarian Notices of Hoxton*, c1870 ms., held in HAD, unpag.

Acknowledgments

I am most grateful to the staff of the Hackney Archives Department who kindly endured request after request for hard to find documents and illustrations. Countless thanks to Claire for editing.

Photograph credits

All reproductions with the kind permission of the Hackney Archives Department except where otherwise indicated.